1981

*French Cinema
of the Occupation
and Resistance*

UNGAR FILM LIBRARY
Stanley Hochman
General Editor

FRENCH CINEMA
OF THE OCCUPATION
AND RESISTANCE

The Birth of a Critical Esthetic

ANDRÉ BAZIN

Collected and with an introduction by
FRANÇOIS TRUFFAUT

TRANSLATED BY STANLEY HOCHMAN

FREDERICK UNGAR PUBLISHING CO. : *New York*

Translator's Dedication
To the memory of
Louis-Avit de Puylaroque

Translated from the original French
Le Cinéma de l'occupation and de la résistance
© 1975 by Union générale d'edition
by arrangement with Janine Bazin

Copyright © 1981 by Frederick Ungar Publishing Co., Inc.
Printed in the United States of America

Library of Congress Cataloging in Publication Data

Bazin, André, 1918–1958.
    French cinema of the occupation and resistance.

    Translation of Le cinéma de l'occupation et de la
résistance.
    1. Moving-pictures—France—Collected works.
    2. Moving-pictures—Reviews. I. Truffaut, François.
    II. Title.
PN1993.5.F7B313   791.43′0944   80–5343
ISBN 0-8044-2022-X

In my work, in what I have been able to accomplish and to learn about myself, André Bazin has been of invaluable assistance: he has perhaps been the greatest and the surest presence.

Federico Fellini

Contents

1 : INTRODUCTION

André Bazin, the Occupation, and I

François Truffaut

I am aware that this book does not offer a complete picture of French cinema under the Occupation; André Bazin did not begin writing until this period was half over, and his material appeared in a student publication that was printed irregularly because of paper restrictions. The texts I have collected here throw light on that period, but they are not a commentary on the Occupation as such—something that was not to become possible until after the Liberation. To tell the truth, it is only now that we have begun to speak objectively about the Occupation and the cinema of that time. It took the salutory shock of *Le Chagrin et la Pitié* (*The Sorrow and the Pity*) and the death of General de Gaulle to make it possible for tongues to become untied and the official, simplistic versions to be abandoned. Above all, we had to wait for the arrival on the scene of new historical researchers who were too young to have been implicated in the events but who were interested enough to undertake their reconstruction: Claude Gauteur, Raymond Borde, Stéphane Levy-Klein, Raymond Chirat, Pierre Guibert, and others. However, to the reader interested in a complete documentation of French cinema from 1940 to 1944 I would recommend—if it weren't out of print—Roger Régent's *Cinéma de France* (Editions Bellefaye, 1948). This is a very detailed work which I often consult and which I hope some publisher will see fit to reissue.

I have subtitled this book "The Birth of a Critical Esthetic," because it seems to me that this was Bazin's real subject. When he wrote his first articles in *L'Echo des Etudiants,* *L'Information Universitaire,* and *Le Courrier de l'Etudiant,* he was twenty-five and had "discovered" cinema only four years before; his favorite film at that moment must have been Marcel Carné's *Le Jour Se Lève* (*Daybreak*), to which after the Liberation he devoted not only his first major essay but also a series of lectures that were delivered in the Paris area and which focused on the theme *How a Film Is Made.* In beginning to write about cinema, Bazin quite naturally asked himself some basic questions about the art of cinematic criticism; it should come as no surprise to note that six of the thirty-odd texts in this collection are reflective essays—"Let's Rediscover Cinema!" "For a Realistic Esthetic," "Toward a Cinematic Criticism," "To Create a Public," "On Realism," and "The Cinema and Popular Art."

Initially, André Bazin intended to be a teacher—he completed his studies at the Ecole Normale Supérieure de Saint-Cloud—and traces of this pedagogical vocation can be seen in his early work. His primary objective is not so much to convince as to encourage reflection. Bazin was always to be more interested in providing a detailed description of a film —what it consists of, how it is made—than in grading or judging it. Because of this, I prefer to speak of him not as the best critic of film but as the best writer on film. This is also the opinion of Eric Rohmer, who on greeting the appearance of the first volume of *Qu'est-ce que le Cinéma?* (*What Is Cinema?*) concluded: "Let us hope that new volumes will be added to the series, because almost all of André Bazin's articles deserve to be republished."

The material collected here, with the help of Janine Bazin, is taken from André Bazin's earliest writings. These little-known texts had become almost unavailable because of the arbitrariness and precariousness that rules over the conservation of press archives on the Occupation. I decided it would be helpful to annotate some of these articles so that the collection as a whole can serve as a working tool for those interested in the cinema of this period. My intention was to augment the informational content of the youthful writing of a man of whom Pierre-Aimé Touchard said at the time: "In ten years André Bazin will be the best film critic in France."

In his very first articles Bazin attacked the easy-going criticism whose complaisance and lack of rigor worried him: "We think that the absence of all effort at systematic thought about cinema of the last fifteen or twenty years [this was written in 1943] is the sign of an abdication whose basic cause may reside in an inability to understand completely the nature of cinema." Bazin was the first to emphasize the necessity of promoting a cinematic culture; he called for an active *cinémathèque* and for film clubs; he became aware—several years before Eric Rohmer, Jacques Rivette, and others who were to rally around him—of the need to analyze cinematic form: "One vainly searches our film reviews for an opinion about the sets, the photography . . . the sound . . . the continuity . . . in a word, for anything about the basic components of cinema."

Just as Maurice Jaubert believed in a popular music, so Bazin believed: "The cinematic esthetic will be social or else cinema will do without an esthetic." At the same time as his first articles were being published, he was the driving force behind the Groupe Cinéma de la Maison des Lettres; he also foresaw that cinema would eventually find a place in the university: "One day we will have an 800-page thesis on the art of comedy in American movies between 1905 and 1917, or something like that. And who then would dare maintain that the subject cannot be taken seriously?"

What Bazin could not foresee is that his own critical work would take on such importance that fifteen years after his death a young student from California, Dudley Andrew, would come to France from the United States to seek out and interview all those who had known him. He spent weeks unearthing Bazin's forgotten texts, and his research led to a master's thesis eventually published in New York as a book! During this same period, Professor Hugh Gray, who was a fellow student of Alfred Hitchcock's at Saint Ignatius in London, interrupted his work on Pindar to translate the Bazin texts collected in *What Is Cinema?*

We now know that André Bazin has won the wager he made when he expressed the hope that in the future, films would be identified by their director or scenario writer rather than by their leading players: "It should be easy, by appealing to the prevalent admiration for competence, to give film credits the place they deserve, and to create, in opposition to the cult of the star, a counter-snobbism of the technician."

All those who were lucky enough to know André Bazin agree in describing him as an astonishing man, a very strong personality, and I have no hesitation in saying that he was, in the most literal sense, an exceptional human being.

André Bazin had the innocence of a character in a Giraudoux play, and his goodness was almost legendary; we sometimes gently made fun of it to hide the emotion it inspired. His illness lasted ten years, the last five of which left no doubt about the eventual outcome, but his extraordinary moral health acted as a counterbalance. Bazin borrowed money openly and lent it without fuss or publicity. Since he thought it absurd and unnatural to ride alone in a car that had place for four, he would often draw up at the Nogent bus stop and offer a lift to three other travelers whom he would then drop off in Paris. When he left Paris for several weeks with Janine and his son Florent, he would phone his friends and lend his house to one and his car to another.

He didn't love only movies; or to be more precise, movies were not a refuge for him, since he also loved life—both people and animals. He had raised all sorts of creatures, from a chameleon to a parrot, to say nothing of a host of squirrels, turtles, a crocodile, and even a Brazilian iguana, which he himself fed with pieces of hardboiled egg impaled on a small stick. Bazin was greatly interested in architecture, and he had written the scenario of a documentary on romanesque churches—published in *Cahiers du Cinéma*—which he would eventually have filmed if his health had improved.

Bazin was a marvelous dialectician, and each of his expositions gave his respondent the impression of seeing logic in action; he believed in the absolute power of discussion and proved it constantly. Even his stuttering helped him, since it made it necessary to listen to him more attentively. So convincing and contagious were his goodness and logic that I have seen people—shopkeepers or policemen—begin a discussion with him in bad faith and in a bad temper and become as a result of the contact with him both honest and logical. Initially, he would adopt the opposing thesis in order to show that he had completely understood it, but then he would refute it with gentleness and precision, leaving the conversation open-ended so as not to impose a conclusion.

In the end, Bazin died without either enemies, adversaries, or detractors, for all the reasons given above and also because his behavior toward others inspired reciprocity; everybody behaved well toward André Bazin, and everybody improved upon contact with him.

Obviously, I didn't know Bazin during the Occupation (I was to meet him in 1947), and my memories of the cinema of that period are only childhood ones, though some of them are quite precise. My first movie memory goes back to 1939, a few months before the Armistice. The scene was the Gaieté Rochechouart, a very large movie theater opposite the Square d'Anvers. The film playing there was *Paradis Perdu* with Micheline Presle, whose beauty and gentleness were extraordinary, and Fernand Gravey. The theater was full of uniformed soldiers on leave accompanied by their young wives or girlfriends. The reader may perhaps remember that Abel Gance's superb melodrama takes place in the period between 1914 and 1935, and that a large part of the film is given over to the war, the trenches, the munitions factories in which women worked, etc. . . . The coincidence between the situation of the characters in the film and that of the spectators was such that the entire audience wept, hundreds of handkerchiefs piercing the darkness with little points of white. Never again was I to feel such an emotional unanimity in response to a film.

It is a well-known fact that periods of war, or simply of poverty and need, increase movie-going. After the Armistice, when the Germans occupied France, movie theaters became a refuge for all, and not only in the figurative sense of the word; they stopped being a refuge when it became the custom to check identity cards at the exits in order to spot young people old enough to be recruited for "French Workers in Germany." As this was not yet my problem, my only anguish about the film was focused on the possibility that its projection might be halted by an air-raid alert: when this happened, you had to leave the theater and, after being given a re-entry ticket, wait in the cellar until the end of the alert.

Until 1942, I never went to the movies unchaperoned, and with the exception of *Paradis Perdu,* I have forgotten the very names of the films I saw. After 1942, and particularly after *Les Visiteurs du Soir (The Devil's Own Envoy)* was released, I got into the habit of going to the movies alone, most often on the sly, to see films of my own choice—or to be more exact, those that were being shown in the eight or ten theaters around Place Pigalle, where I lived. At some other time and place, I will relate my memories about playing hookey to go to the movies; all I want to do here is re-create the cinematic ambiance of the Occupation so that Bazin's texts can be seen in the light of the period.

Every morning I would run out to buy the daily *Aujourd'hui* read by my parents and open it to the theater page to satisfy my curiosity. There was much discussion about actor Alain Cuny, who was the delight of the chansonniers. The slowness of his delivery was remarked on: "Grass springs up between the lines," commented one critic; "If you want to catch the last Métro, you'd better not go to hear Alain Cuny," said another. Alain Cuny was also enjoying a triumph in *Les Visiteurs du Soir* (the longest first-run of that period), but this time it was the white chateau dreamed up by Alexandre Trauner that was the target of the sarcasms: "A cardboard chateau . . . a papier-mâché Middle Ages . . ." Marcel Carné defended himself by explaining logically that it was

When the white chateau designed by Alexandre Trauner for *Les Visi-*
teurs du Soir (1942) was criticized for looking so spanking new, director
Carné pointed out that in medieval France such chateaux were inevitably new. (French Cultural Services)

necessary for such chateaux to be new! I also remember one of the leading critics praising Michel Bouquet and his irreproachable diction: "If he were to muff a line, the theater would collapse."

My aunt, who was studying the violin at the Conservatoire, had become friendly with the head of the cosmetic department at the Galleries Lafayette department store, where he sold under-the-counter copies of the French translation of *Gone with the Wind,* the sale of which was forbidden, as was that of most English and American novels.

As Louis Aragon points out in his poem "L'Affiche Rouge," the walls of the Métro were plastered with posters calling for the denunciation of people wanted by the authorities; because of this it was impossible not to be shocked by the advertisements for the film *Vautrin,* adapted from Balzac by Pierre Billon. They featured actor Michel Simon and the words: "Wanted, an escaped convict . . ."

In 1943, if I had been six or seven years older, I would perhaps have been one of the readers of *L'Echo des Etudiants* and I would have agreed with the following observation by Bazin: "I am, perhaps, going to scandalize some readers by saying that of all French artistic activities since the war, the cinema is the only one that is making progress."

In truth, French cinema was extremely active during the war. The dance halls were closed, it was cold at home, people left the city only to look for food on the farms, and, at least where Paris was concerned, the movie theaters were never empty. Stairway windows had been daubed with laundry blueing, apartment windows had to be blacked out, and a local volunteer known as a "sector warden" patrolled the streets to make sure that blackout regulations were being observed; if light trickled out of a window, he would blow a warning note on his whistle. No monument was illuminated, and especially not the Eiffel Tower. In short, the Germans and the Pétain government wanted to be sure that Paris could not be spotted from the air. This in no way prevented the English, in 1943, from bombing the La Chapelle quarter and especially the immense Dufayel warehouse on rue de Clignancourt, where I don't know what was stored. Paris could in truth no longer be called the City of Light; anybody who went out at night provided himself with a small flashlight that he would turn on when he left the Métro exit and keep on until he got home so as not to stumble along the sidewalk. As I remember it, the Sacha Guitry film *Donne-moi Tes Yeux* (!) is the only one to give a faithful idea of blackout reality.

As an example of the strictness with which blackout regulations were observed, I need only note that it was by no means rare to hear couples making love in the streets, standing in front of apartment house doors. Unfortunately, my young age at the time allows me to testify only to what I could hear.

In order not to abandon the topic of sex too quickly and to nevertheless return to the topic of cinema, I will add the curious testimony of a school friend whose mother was an usher at the Gaumont-Palace—that great hulk that was for several years to remain the largest movie theater in Europe. During the Occupation, people went to the Gaumont-Palace to hear, between film showings, popular tunes arranged for the organ by Van Horbecke "and his orchestra"; after the Liberation—Van Horbecke having been "purified"—people returned to gauge, as connoisseurs, the legs of the Bluebell Girls! Anyway, my friend, who the following year was to drown at a summer camp, swore that his mother and her co-workers would collect no less than sixty pairs of panties in the loges and in the spaces between the rows after the last Sunday showing. Was this information authentic or was the whole thing a myth? Why consider it suspect when it came from the son of an usher—a seater, one might say, who was herself well sited to know the truth? And yet, when it is remembered that during the war even the smallest piece of cloth required the surrender of ration coupons . . . but perhaps not for underwear? Anyhow, what absentmindedness . . . and what passion! In short, I need hardly add that those sixty weekly pairs of panties—we never failed to check the exact number every week and it rarely varied by more than ten—made us dream of things that had nothing to do with either cinematic art or Bazin's ideas.

Since most often I would illegally sneak into the movie theater, generally with the help of a pal—he would pay his way and then once inside open a fire exit so that I could slip in—I had to spend the intermission* locked in the john, waiting for the house lights to go out so that I could find a seat in the dark. Sometimes I had to wait until the newsreels had been shown, because to prevent them from being booed or razzed, they were not projected in the dark. From these long enforced sessions in the john, I have preserved the memory of a patriotic grafitto, which despite being only relatively humorous, has remained engraved in my memory.

> *Adolf Hitler, the world's killer*
> *Will find winter a lot chiller*

It was a few weeks before the Battle of Stalingrad.

Another memory, this one more sinister, concerns the film credits on which certain names had been scratched out or blacked over so as to render them illegible; the idea was to eliminate the name of so and so, who had worked on the film—a Jew. The situation of Jews in the movie industry was by no means enviable. Those who hadn't the money to leave France were better off remaining under cover; some managed to work under false names, as did the set designer Trauner or the composer Joseph Kosma, who worked on Marcel Carné films by allowing their contributions to be signed by others.

Not every film critic was called André Bazin or Jacques

---

* In French movie theaters, there is an intermission between the coming attractions and advertisements, and the feature film. —Trans.

Audiberti, and one of the most famous, the writer Lucien Rebatet—who under the pseudonym François Vinneuil did the film reviews for *Je Suis Partout*—went at it with a heavy hand in his book *Les Tribus du Cinéma et du Theatre* (The Tribes of the Cinema and of the Theater) published by N.E.F. in April 1941 as part of a series called *Les Juifs en France* (The Jews in France). Lucien Rebatet gave the signal for the witchhunt: "In theory all cinematic activity is forbidden to Jews. They don't seem to be very alarmed by this. They find reassurance in the official accomplices they always manage to recruit. Whatever is undertaken or decided in favor of French cinema, the first thing to be done is to de-Jew it." Further on, Rebatet spells out the program: "Sooner or later our soil will have to be cleared of several hundred thousand Jews, beginning with Jews without regular papers, those who are not naturalized, those who have most recently arrived, those whose political and financial malfeasance is most obvious—in other words all the Jews working in cinema. Before this is done, we will pick out those for whom exile would be too benign a punishment and who will have to pay their debt with prison terms at least. In the meantime the entire French film industry, from the production to the printing of films to the management of the smallest theater, will have to be inexorably and definitively closed to Jews without distinction of either class or origin."

As is generally the case with racists, Rebatet injects sexuality into his *passion* (to use Sartre's terminology): "But the Jews in cinema are not content to offend us by their ugliness and by buying the prettiest girls in Paris." And here is a sample of Rebatet in an impartial and objective mood: "It would be absurd to try to hide all that cinema owes to the half-Jew Charlie Chaplin. No one has ever thought of denying that a Jew can have genius, especially when the Christian blood in his veins manages—very rarely, it's true—to correct his racial heredity." Then Lucien Rebatet enlarges his scope: "It should be noted that several directors, and by no means the least of

them, such as Julien Duvivier, are married to Jewesses and
held by them in the claws of Israel. As for the others, they are
taking a holiday."

To tell the truth, they were not all taking a holiday, but
understandably, "Aryans" such as Duvivier, Renoir, and René
Clair had preferred to take the boat to New York and then the
plane to Hollywood [1] before the arrival of the Germans
and the triumph of Rebatet, who further on in his book goes
after the most prestigious director of the period: "Marcel
Carné is an Aryan. But he has been impregnated by all the
Jewish influences and he owes his success to the Jews; he has
been fussed over by them, all his works have been shot under their banners . . . I don't set myself up for a moralist.
True artists should be free to depict the worst crimes. But
Carné and his Jews have made French cinema wallow in a
fatalism, a determinism, that is degrading."

The Rebatet-Vinneuil of 1941 can hardly be accused of
being ideologically inconsistent, for three years earlier in *Action Française* (April 29, 1938) he had written about *La
Marseillaise*: "Henceforth, in speaking of a political film by
M. Jean Renoir if I have to praise 'the artist,' I will remember to recall in every line that in a true French state 'the
citizen' would be liable to imprisonment in a concentration
camp."

I have, perhaps, quoted at too great a length from this
book by Rebatet because it cannot be found today and because it is useful to see what happens when circumstances
place extremists near the seats of power and they experience
an irresistible temptation to pass from theory to practice.
After the Liberation, the Comité d'Epuration du Cinéma
(Committee for Purification of the Cinema) was in its turn to
exercise this sort of Rebatism.[2] Certain directors and certain
actors were to decide that other directors and other actors
would be banned "for life." (In practice this amounted to
two or three years of enforced idleness.) It is difficult not to see

in these settlings of accounts within a single profession confused intentions that make them, at the very least, suspect.

For example, all during the war the fame of Pierre Fresnay kept growing while that of Pierre Blanchar diminished. After the Liberation, however, it was learned that Pierre Blanchar was the author of one of the articles in the underground press that denounced *Le Corbeau* (*The Raven*) as anti-French and that the same Pierre Blanchar was to preside over the Comité d'Epuration, which was to decide that Pierre Fresnay would no longer have the right to appear on a stage. Pierre Fresnay was to be joined in prison for several weeks or several months by Sacha Guitry, Tino Rossi, Albert Préjean, Arletty, Robert Le Vigan. Those among the "purified" who were permitted to go back to work were given a "reprimand posted in the place of work"—in other words on the walls of the studio.

This grating of the wheels in the mill of patriotism was to be well described by Jean Paulhan in his "Letter to the Leaders of the Resistance": "It is to the others that I am speaking. It is especially to those who took part in the Resistance. Can't they see that they have been caught in the trap? That they have decided that they are members of the Resistance forever more: pure, saved? That they have fallen lower than those whom they condemn? No, they are so proud of having one day found themselves on the right side that they have become moralists."

I believe that Marcel Ophuls' film *Le Chagrin et la Pitié*—despite attacks on it from all sides, and despite the fact that French television still refuses to show it so as not to chagrin those who had been pitiless—is the film that describes with the greatest exactitude and good faith the spectrum of French behavior in the 1940–45 period.

But to get back to the prosperity of French cinema during the war, it might be attributed to several factors besides the strong need for escape and entertainment experienced by a population deprived of heat, transportation, dancing . . . and food. For the first time in the history of cinema there was no competition from American films. Many German films were shown, and some of them, like Veit Harlan's *Golden City* or Joseph von Baky's *The Adventures of Baron Munchausen,* were quality productions; but the others weren't very attractive. There were also some Italian films, and a few of them, like Alessandro Blasetti's *The Iron Crown,* were rather delirious; but French films were the main attraction—so much so that they paid for themselves by exhibition in France alone, something very rare in our own time.

The departure from France of five leading directors—Renoir, Clair, Ophuls, Feyder, and Duvivier [3]; the detention in prison camps of others; the enforced idleness of Jewish filmmakers—all of this contributed to the arrival on the scene of a certain number of new directors whom nobody ever thought of labeling the "new wave" even if that was what it was. In a profession more and more closed to young people since the invention of sound and the increased costs that went along with it, one suddenly saw some twenty-five new filmmakers promoted to the rank of directors—some of whom, like playwright Jean Anouilh, were already famous in other fields. Some had been young scriptwriters—Albert Valentin, André Cayatte, H.-G. Clouzot; some, assistants—Louis Daquin, André Zwoboda, Jacques Becker, Claude Autant-Lara; some, actors—René Lefèvre, Pierre Blanchar, or editors—Le Hénaff, Jean Delannoy; and, let's not forget an outsider—Robert Bresson, whose first directorial assignment, *Les Anges du Péché* (*Angels of the Streets*), has probably remained the best film of this period.

In August 1940, at Marseilles, Marcel Pagnol, thanks to his independent and artisanal organization, became the first to return to filming: *La Fille du Puisatier* (*The Well-Digger's Daughter*), with Raimu and Fernandel. Four years later, the last two films of the Occupation were to be begun before the Liberation, interrupted by electricity cutbacks, and finished after the war: Robert Bresson's *Les Dames du Bois de Boulogne* (*Ladies of the Park*) and Marcel Carné's *Les Enfants du Paradis* (*Children of Paradise*).

By drawing on the irreproachable documentation of Roger Régent's book, I have compiled the following list of interesting films made during the Occupation:

Marcel Pagnol—*La Fille du Puisatier*

Abel Gance—*Vénus Aveugle, Le Capitaine Fracasse*

Jean Grémillon—*Remorques, Lumière d'Eté, Le Ciel Est à Vous*

Jacques Becker—*Dernier Atout, Goupi Mains Rouges, Falbalas*

Louis Daquin—*Nous les Gosses, Le Voyageur de la Toussaint, Madame et le Mort, Premier de Cordée*

Sacha Guitry—*Désirée Clary, Donne-moi Tes Yeux, La Malibran*

Georges Lacombe—*Le Dernier des Six, L'Escalier sans Fin, Florence Est Folle, Montmartre-sur-Seine, Le Journal Tombe à Cinq Heures, Monsieur la Souris*

H.-G. Clouzot—*L'Assassin Habite au 21, Le Corbeau*

Henri Decoin—*Premier Rendez-vous, Les Inconnus dans la Maison, L'Homme de Londres, Le Bienfaiteur, Je Suis avec Toi, Mariage d'Amour*

Christian-Jaque—*L'Assassinat du Père Noël, La Symphonie Fantastique, Voyage sans Espoir, Carmen, Sortilèges, Premier Bal*

Jacques de Baroncelli—*La Duchesse de Langeais, Ce N'est pas Moi, Haut le Vent, Les Mystères de Paris, Le Pavillon Brûle*

Roland Tual—*Le Lit à Colonnes, Bonsoir Mesdames, Bonsoir Messieurs*

Marcel Carné—*Les Visiteurs du Soir*

Jean Delannoy—*L'Eternel Retour, Pontcarral, Le Bossu, Fièvres*

Claude Autant-Lara—*Le Mariage de Chiffon, Douce, Lettres d'Amour*

Serge de Poligny—*Le Baron Fantôme, La Fiancée des Ténèbres*

Marc Allégret—*Félicie, Nanteuil, L'Arlésienne, La Belle Aventure, Lunegarde, Les Petites du Quai aux Fleurs*

André Cayatte—*Pierre et Jean, La Fausse Maîtresse, Au Bonheur des Dames, Le Dernier Sou*

Pierre Billon—*Vautrin, L'Inévitable Monsieur Dubois, Mademoiselle X, Le Soleil A Toujours Raison*

Léo Joannon—*Le Camion Blanc, Caprice, Le Carrefour des Enfants Perdus, Lucrèce*

Albert Valentin—*A la Belle Frégate, La Maison des Sept Jeunes Filles, Marie Martine, La Vie de Plaisir*

Jean Dréville—*Les Affaires Sont les Affaires, Annette et la Dame Blonde, Le Cadet de l'Océan, La Cage aux Rossignols, Tornavara, Les Roquevillard*

Maurice Tourneur—*Cécile Est Morte, La Main du Diable, Mamz'elle Bonaparte, Péchés de Jeunesse, Le Val d'Enfer*

Marcel L'Herbier—*Histoire de Rire, L'Honorable Catherine, Une Vie de Bohème, La Nuit Fantastique*

There were also other films signed by Pierre Prévert, Henri Fescourt, René Lefèvre, Jean Faurez, Lèon Poirier, Guillaume Radot, and Léon Mathot. The complete list would be too long to reprint here, and I must add that my memories are vague about those films I was unable to resee after the Liberation.

There was no place for subversion or protest in the films of this period; the sanctions imposed would have gone beyond those of the Commission de Censure. I have noted above the extent to which a director like Marcel Carné was restricted to a "supervised liberty" under the eye of Rebatet-Vinneuil. It is therefore understandable that cinema took refuge in historical films and films of fantasy and enchantment; and it is also understandable that the extraordinary success (mixed with controversy) of *Les Visiteurs du Soir* was followed by the initiation of production on *La Fiancée des Ténèbres, Le Baron Fantôme, L'Eternel Retour,* and *Sortilèges.*[4]

Nevertheless I cannot accept the sometimes espoused patriotic theory that the historical or fantasy films made during this period deliberately delivered a courageous message coded in favor of the Resistance [5]; however, for those who criticize the apolitical and escapist cinema of the Occupation I would like to cite Rogert Régent: "Though among these 220 films shot under such disastrous conditions there are many mediocre ones, at least we can be proud not to have seen a single French producer worthy of that name consent to make so much as one propaganda film in favor of the enemy. We all know in what direction such propaganda tended!"

It might also be added—for the benefit of those who complain that present-day French cinema pays too little attention to political questions and who compare it to its disadvantage with Italian protest cinema—that it would be well to remember, without pushing the comparison too far, that Italian cinema of 1940–44 was almost entirely pro-Mussolini and fascist, whereas 98 percent of French cinema during the Occupation managed not to be Pétainist.

To sum up, at the time of the Liberation there was an interesting and ambitious French cinema that had renewed itself by opening itself to young and new talents. The Blum-Byrnes agreements within the framework of the Marshall Plan, allowing for the importation of a great number of American films, was to make the situation of French cinema very difficult. As it might be said today, the French film was no longer "competitive." A "Committee for the Defense of French Cinema" staged a demonstration in which actors and directors demanded a limit on the number of American films shown in France. As for the film industry unions, they hardened their positions, discouraged the advent of new directors, and tried to keep Jean-Pierre Melville from shooting *Le Silence de la Mer* with a reduced crew—the same conditions as Italian neo-realism operated under.

In the name of truth it has to be said that the established directors did not seem at all eager to favor the promotion of their younger colleagues. Whereas twenty-five new directors had had the opportunity to make their debuts during the four years of the Occupation—among them Becker, Bresson, and Clouzot—in the fourteen years between 1945 and 1959 (the beginning of the New Wave) the only new names were René Clément, Jacques Tati, Jean-Pierre Melville, Roger Leenhardt, Yves Ciampi, Alexandre Astruc, and Marcel Camus. The numerical disproportion is obvious.

Nevertheless, this disappointing postwar period saw the birth of a new criticism under the prompting of André Bazin, a better informed and more responsible criticism which he had himself called into being and defined in one of his first articles: "We believe that criticism is indispensable to the development and future of cinema. . . . One would think that like the intangible shadows on the screen, this unusual art has no past, leaves no traces, has no depth. It is more than time to invent a criticism in relief."

Present-day French cinema is the heir to this "criticism in relief" because it was born of the thought and reflection of André Bazin.

François Truffaut
(1975)

Notes

1. In Hollywood, Duvivier, Clair, and Renoir were, if not awaited, at least already known and appreciated, thanks to the success of *Un Carnet de Bal, Sous les Toits de Paris* (*Under the Roofs of Paris*), and *La Grande Illusion* (*Grand Illusion*). They could therefore reasonably hope to find work, in other words, to make films. Not all the French directors were in the same situation.

2. Lucien Rebatet was to spend ten years in prison, which he left with a handsome, fat novel, *Les Deux Etendards*. Using the name Vinneuil, he began contributing film articles to various publications; under his real name he did a political column in *Rivarol*.

3. Except for Feyder, who went to Switzerland, the others settled in Hollywood, as did Leonide Moguy, Diamant-Berger, Michèle Morgan, Jean Gabin, Dalio and his wife, Madeleine Lebeau, Victor Francen, and Jean-Pierre Aumont.

4. Curiously enough, the success of *Les Visiteurs du Soir*, for which the scenario was written by Jacques Prévert, was particularly helpful to Jean Cocteau, who made a strong comeback at the time as a scenario writer (*L'Eternel Retour, Le Baron Fantôme,* and *Les Dames du Bois de Boulogne*), which in turn probably facilitated his return to direction (*La Belle et la Bête, 1945*).

5. To be fair, I should point out an observation by Roger Régent about Jean Delannoy's *Pontcarral, Colonel d'Empire*. In that film, Pierre Blanchar played a Napoleonic colonel hostile to the July Monarchy. When he told the interrogating judge that "under such a regime, sir, it is an honor to be condemned!" Occupation audiences regularly applauded the line.

2 : FRENCH FILMS
UNDER THE OCCUPATION

Let's Rediscover Cinema!

"Can one take an interest in cinema?" a journalist once asked Paul Souday. Response: "No, a serious critic cannot take an interest in cinema because cinema is less than goat dung." How many students who don't have all the excuses of the eminent drama critic more or less basically agree with this![1]

We could once more place the intellectuals of the modern world on trial, denouncing them for their ignorance of the most important esthetico-social development since the Middle Ages, for their refusal to believe in anything not consecrated by a bookish and academic tradition, for their suspicion of an art that cannot help but appeal to the masses: *odi profanum vulgus* . . . For the moment, however, we are going to try to plead extenuating circumstances.

To begin with, a little history: intellectuals have not always manifested our contemptuous indifference toward the cinema. Indeed, it was the "serious" literary types—even academicians—who even before the surrealist poets, unhesitatingly bent solicitously over the cradle of this Gargantua. The truth is, however, that more than a quarter of a century after the disastrous experience of "Films d'Art," cinema has not yet recovered from their brief reign. . . . Nevertheless, their intentions were honorable.

After the war,[2] "serious critics" no longer believed in the rapscallion, but a lively and abundant magazine literature came to be born around silent film, and at the same time "cinema clubs" were established in several avant-garde movie theaters. The incontestable influence of this cinematic elite did a great deal to help silent films attain their esthetic and technical polish, and even to prolong the concern with style for several years after the sound revolution. But the clubs were unable to avoid the reef of intellectualism, and they very quickly became walled in by a subtle estheticism

25

which was interesting in itself but risked leading cinema along paths foreign to its basic sociological laws.

The amazing disaffection of this elite several years after the disappearance of silent films (a disaffection that is borne out by the decline in cinematic literature after 1934–36) can perhaps be explained by their disappointment at seeing the cinema over which they had exercised a direct influence escape it in the technical, economic, and human revolution brought about by sound. . . .

Let us also add that for many, because of this intransigent estheticism, sound could be only a factor of realism and facileness, the beginning of decadence.

In any case, it is clear in 1943 that this generation of clubs totally abandoned the struggle without passing on the torch. Young people today, and perhaps especially intellectual young people, know absolutely nothing about cinema, ask themselves no questions about it, and express an opinion about it only to despise it. But there may be some excuse for them. To the responsibility of their elders, who abdicated and did nothing to transmit an enthusiasm that had become shameful, must be added historical circumstances whose importance has not yet been pointed out. These young people have known only a stabilized cinema, one ensconced in an enervating technical security, henceforth in possession of realistic means that make possible all kinds of easy ways out, all kinds of laziness, when these means should, on the contrary, have called for a style that was more spare, more austere. They did not witness the birth of cinema, they did not know the intoxication of its future—that ambiance of conquest which surrounded this growing Seventh Art; they did not live through its history.

No doubt they should have studied this history, just as they did that of theater and poetry. Indeed, all culture implies the knowledge of a past, a past which we begin learning as soon as we enter school. It is here, however, that we touch on the very heart of the problem.

This art, which is only a few decades old, has left us no documentation. The literary residue left by the theater is enough to enable us in the present to judge a tragedy by Euripides; the technical, economic, and political restraints on cinema make it all but impossible to study a film produced only ten years ago. Whereas technical progress has permitted the recent popularization of music and painting by means of records and reproductions, it seems that only cinema, the result of all this technical progress, must remain its prisoner.

The previous generation, having lived through the history of film, did not suffer from this lack; its memory served as a cinémathèque. Young people today, however, are the first of the generations who will know less and less about cinema even as they go to the movies more and more often.

Isn't it obvious to all that under these conditions an art inevitably falls into decadence? It can only, slowly but surely, follow the downward path toward facileness, submit to all the laws of gravity. Let us, in fact, be wary of believing that cinema is just beginning and therefore still full of promise. It may, perhaps, no longer be at its technical beginning, but it is surely no longer at its esthetic beginning, and the curve of its stylistic evolution already shows a downward path. If steps are not taken to furnish it with an educated public—the condition essential for all artistic life—the time will come when the very idea of a decadence will have no meaning for any moviegoer in the world. At that moment the late Seventh Art will have definitively given way to a cinematic industry enjoying enormous prosperity.

The very existence of the cinema as an art therefore requires that our generation reconstitute an educated public that has enough technical and historic awareness to create a critical ambiance for a work, to affirm the hierarchies, to judge the effort of the creator.

While waiting for a chair in cinema and for courses in which films can be examined critically, and more realistically, while waiting for a functioning cinémathèque, couldn't we ask of students that they develop a greater awareness of what cinema is?

Think of the extraordinary spectacle offered us: the birth of an art which is as important by virtue of its esthetic innovation—the depiction of movement—as by its social consequences, unprecedented since the invention of printing and the banning of performances of the *mystères*. Will we turn our backs on this prodigious development because it is contemporary? Will we be so blind to our own times? Will we continue to limit our humanism and our culture to written civilization because we are accustomed to confusing it with all civilization?

The world is developing, and art is creating itself—an art which must be maintained, against the reel merchants and the mere ticket buyers, in the vigor of its youth and in its healthiest popular exigencies. Let's finally become aware of it. Let's rediscover cinema!   (June 26, 1943)

Notes

1. This article, like most of those that follow, appeared in *L'Echo des Etudiants*. I will indicate the date of publication of each article, but I will only give the source if it does not come from *L'Echo des Etudiants, L'Information Universitaire,* or *Courrier de l'Etudiant.* (F.T.)

2. Bazin wrote this in 1943. He was obviously speaking of World War 1. (F.T.)

Pierre Prévert's Adieu Léonard

Adieu . . . Prévert! We suspected that an entire film signed Prévert would not be a complete success, but we were savoring its faults in advance. *Drôle de Drame* [1] was in its time also an example of those errors that are a hundred times richer in intelligence and instruction than most successful productions. We knew the temptations to which Prévert's dialogue could succumb, but at least they didn't include awkwardness and banality. We didn't even reproach him for *Lumière d'Eté*,[2] despite its bottom-of-the-barrel scrapings of Prévertian wit. Alas, how disappointed we were not to find in *Adieu Léonard* [3] even the charm of his usual sins. This time the problem isn't Prévert's faults but the absence, a painful absence, of all his good qualities. What! Prévert give us this series of misfired gags, this heavy, overemphasized, and predictable fantasy that is hardly worthy of M. Yves Mirande? The very fact that some were ecstatic about this scenario proves the extent to which the possibilities of cinema have been forgotten, because if the film did contain an idea, that idea could only have been brought out by the style in which the film was made; this whimsical and slightly insane satire could live only in a universe in which the rhythm and poetry of the images had imposed a probability superior to the improbability. Here, however, we never shake off the demands of logic; we never voluntarily accept the world that is offered us. Think of the satirical humor of *You Can't Take It with You*,[4] of which *Adieu Léonard* often seems a bad imitation: that was cinema! And what rhythm! Here, on the contrary, the overall design of the film is awkward and slow enough to inspire despair, and the editing painstakingly underscores the failures of intentions (the business about the plate of mushrooms, for example, might have lent itself to something wonderful). Add to this a clumsiness, a constant awkwardness of the characters, who seem unwilling to enter into their own game. Nobody can believe in it, not even the little birds. We're willing to allow that the incredible nullity of Charles Trenet may explain some of this, but his co-players scarcely involve us any more. Only Carette sometimes manages; the others, including Brasseur, carry on like boring puppets. It's not their fault, because only two people are responsible for this venture: Pierre and Jacques.[5]

To forget it, we went—for the fourth time—to see *Le Jour Se Lève*. Bonjour Prévert!   (October 9, 1943)

Notes

1. Directed by Marcel Carné (1937). Scenario and dialogue by Jacques Prévert.

2. Directed by Jean Grémillon (1942).

3. *Adieu Léonard* (originally entitled *L'Honorable Léonard*). Direction: Pierre Prévert. Music: Joseph Kosma (clandestinely signed Georges Mouqué). Actors: Charles Trenet, Maurice Baquet, Roger Blin, Jacqueline Pagnol, Pierre Brasseur, Delmont, Jacques Dufilho, Julien Carette, Mouloudji.

4. Directed by Frank Capra (1938).

5. Beginning in 1933, Jacques Prévert had been the scenarist or adaptor-dialoguist of Autant-Lara's *Ciboulette* (1933); Marc Allégret's *L'Hôtel du Libre Echange* (1933); Autant-Lara's *My Partner Mr. Davis* (1934); Richard Pottier's *Un Oiseau Rare* (1935); Jean Stelli's *Jeunesse d'Abord* (1935); Jean Renoir's *Le Crime de Monsieur Lange* (1935); Marcel Carné's *Jenny* (1936); René Sti's *Montonnet* (1936); Marcel Carné's *Drôle de Drame* (1937); Marcel Carné's *Quai des Brumes* (1938); Christian-Jaque's *Ernest le Rebelle* (1938); Marcel Carné's *Le Jour Se Lève* (1939); Jean Grémillon's *Remorques* (1939); Pierre Billon's *Le Soleil A Toujours Raison* (1941); Marcel Carné's *Les Visiteurs du Soir* (1942); Jean Grémillon's *Lumière d'Eté* (1943).

Before directing *Adieu Léonard* in 1943, his brother, Pierre Prévert, had been the director and co-scenarist with Jacques of *L'Affaire Est dans le Sac* (1932), and then of various shorts.

Panorama of the Past Season

What had been true of the theater was also true of cinema. The past seasons had left us very disappointed, close to despair about French cinema. Except for two or three films, sometimes partially or totally shot before the Armistice, the average seemed obliged to establish itself at the intellectual and sentimental level that safely assures the reel merchants a return on their money.

Marcel Carné's *Les Visiteurs du Soir* [1] was the first to give us new hope. This film can be considered the most interesting effort to raise cinema to the level of poetic expression since the war. In the unchallenged context of ambient idiocy, Carné's film burst like a provocation. This required courage, because if the public is not by nature as stupid as too many producers imagine, it does particularly dislike having its habits disturbed. Those who are among the first to upset it, run the risk of paying heavily, to the benefit of competitors who then safely pass through the breech opened in the wall of conventionalism. Even if *Les Visiteurs du Soir* doesn't have all the merits that a rightly unanimous criticism has bestowed on it, even if in perspective this film appears to have partially fallen short of its ambitions, we can never be sufficiently grateful to it for having restored to French cinema a grandeur and style which it seemed to have renounced.

Critical precision obliges us to speak of film production after *Les Visiteurs du Soir*. Because the cinema has neither specialized publics nor theaters, one too easily forgets to establish the necessary hierarchies among the cinematic genres. A good comedy cannot be measured against a tragedy. Edouard Bourdet's *Père* cannot be compared to Henry de Montherlant's *La Reine Morte*. It should thus be clearly understood that thanks to its spiritual value the film most in the public eye is vastly superior to other productions even though these may be perfectly justified within their own genre.

Marcel Carné had long since proven his talent. But what was new about the 1943 season was that it revealed, or at least decisively forced upon our attention, young directors.

Claude Autant-Lara [2] gave us *Mariage de Chiffon* and *Lettres d'Amour*. Becker,[3] whose *Dernier Atout* had shown his technical skill, assured himself of a durable and justified success with *Goupi Mains Rouges,* a work of almost perfectly uniform quality, of a firm and precise style in which the mastery of the director unhesitatingly asserts itself.

Daquin,[4] who made his debut in 1941 with *Nous les Gosses,* partially missed the boat with *Le Voyageur de la Toussaint,* taken from a Georges Simenon novel, in which admirable qualities of detail and an extremely sure and delicate sense of cinematic expression have been compromised by an overly slow continuity and by errors in the use of decor. We hope that *Premier de Cordée* will be an achievement worthy of this director. Jean Grémillon had previously given us *Remorques,* a superior work spoiled by heartbreaking errors in the mise-en-scène. Our pleasure in *Lumière d'Eté* was all the greater, therefore, because that film demonstrated a faultless technical assurance. Very uneven as to the scenario, the film is a little anthology of cinematic expression from the point of view of its dramatic, plastic, and sound qualities.

As for the veterans, Marcel L'Herbier proved with *L'Honorable Catherine* that French-style comedy can get away from filmed vaudeville and is on a level with foreign production insofar as overall design and rhythm are concerned.

We have saved for the end the final two revelations of the year: Bresson and Clouzot. Bresson was admirably seconded by cameraman Agostini in *Les Anges du Péché,* in which Giraudoux revealed qualities as a dialoguist that we had previously glimpsed in *La Duchesse de Langeais.*[5] Henceforth, alongside the novelist and the playwright, we will have to consider a third Giraudoux, a Giraudoux capable of a spareness and sobriety of style that keeps us agreeably surprised. Are we about to see a "literary" cinema take its place alongside the theater, a cinema whose scripts and dialogue are worthy of publication? And finally Clouzot, who—like Becker —had his baptism of fire in detective films, showed us with

Le Corbeau [6] that he is capable of raising this genre of mechanical intrigue to a high level of human expression.

We acknowledge the injustice of not citing all the credits on these films. The problem of the auteur of a film has not been resolved and cannot be *a priori*. The contribution of the cameraman varies with the film, and therefore the director cannot always be considered the sole creator. Cinema is an art of teamwork. Each film requires that the critic make an individual judgment as to its auteurs. It is therefore important to at least note the role of the scenarist and the dialoguist. Let us merely point out that Georges Simenon and Pierre Véry have shown themselves to be the French novelists most directly adaptable to the screen and that the 1943 season is indebted to them for more than one good story.[7] Overall, however, we have not had, insofar as scenario and dialogue are concerned, the same revelations that we have had from the point of view of direction. Except for those by Laroche and Aurenche, who are not exactly novices, no name can be added to those of Spaak and Prévert. Let us also note that as for the latter, the disastrous experience of *Adieu Léonard* has shown that it was further than we thought from the dialogue to the scenario and from the scenario to the mise-en-scène. The competition organized by Comoedia-Gaumont has—alas!—confirmed a weakness that we hope is not congenital: the inability of French intellectuals to be cinematically inventive.

We are unable to give the documentary and the animated cartoon the space they deserve. It is perhaps in these minor genres that the Direction de la Cinématographie Nationale has shown itself most consistently effective. It was not, indeed, a question of safeguarding a tradition, but of starting from scratch in a domain that the prewar cinema had either abandoned or in which it had dishonored itself.

Despite the uneasiness that the scenario crisis may give rise to, the season just ending is among the more reassuring.

To those who object that it has not revealed great creative artists but only skillful craftsmen, it would be easy to reply that the last ten years have seen only the stars of Renoir and Carné [8] rise. It's not every year that you discover a Feyder.[9] The fact that in the midst of ever-increasing difficulties French cinema was able to produce in a few months six or seven works of such quality proves, it would seem, more than its vitality—its veritable will to rebirth; and it testifies that this cinema has the artistic and technical personnel to bring it off.   (October 23, 1943)

Notes

1. Marcel Carné, the filmmaker most often cited in this book, was born on August 18, 1909. A movie journalist, he became assistant to René Clair and to Jacques Feyder. His first feature film was *Jenny* (1936), for which Jacques Prévert wrote the dialogue and Joseph Kosma the music. In the following years he made *Drôle de Drame* (1937), *Quai des Brumes* (1938), *Hôtel du Nord* (1938), and *Le Jour Se Lève* (1939).

2. Claude Autant-Lara, who before the war had made several films in collaboration with Maurice Lehmann, made his real debut as director in 1941 with *Le Mariage de Chiffon,* taken from a novel by Gyp and starring Odette Joyeux, whom he again directed in *Lettres d'Amour* (1942) with François Périer, and later in *Douce* (1943), from a novel by Michel Davet.

3. Jacques Becker, assistant to Jean Renoir from 1928 (*Le Bled*) until 1937 (*La Grande Illusion*), made his debut with *L'Or du Cristobal* (1939—never completed). His first real film was therefore *Dernier Atout* (1942), with Raymond Rouleau, Mireille Balin, and Pierre Renoir. It was followed by *Goupi Mains Rouges* (1943), from the novel by Pierre Véry with Fernand Ledoux, Blanchette Brunoy, Robert Le Vigan, Georges Rollin Albert Rémy (Grand Prix du Cinéma Français, 1943).

4. Louis Daquin, assistant to Pierre Chenal, Abel Gance, and Jean Grémillon, made his debut in 1941 with *Nous les Gosses,* which was followed by *Madame et le Mort* (1942), *Le Voyageur de la Toussaint* (1942), and *Premier de Cordée* (1943).

5. Directed by Jacques de Baroncelli, it was taken from the novel by Balzac and starred Edwige Feuillère and Pierre-Richard Wilm.

6. H.-G. Clouzot's first film was *L'Assassin Habite au 21* (1941). *Le Corbeau* had a scenario by Louis Chavance, who collaborated with Clouzot on the adaptation and dialogue. The film starred Pierre Fres-

nay, Ginette Leclerc, Pierre Larquey, Micheline Francey, Louis Seigner, Roger Blin, Noël Roquevert, and Sylvie.

7. Between 1939 and 1943, Pierre Véry wrote (or collaborated on): *L'Enfer des Anges* and *L'Assassinat du Père Noël,* by Christian-Jaque; *Pension Jonas,* by Pierre Caron; *Mélodie pour Toi,* by Willy Rozier; *L'Assassin A Peur la Nuit,* by Jean Delannoy; *Madame et le Mort,* by Louis Daquin; *Goupi Main Rouges,* by Jacques Becker. During that same period, the works of Georges Simenon that reached the screen included: *Le Voyageur de la Toussaint,* by Louis Daquin; *La Maison des Sept Jeunes Filles,* by Albert Valentin; *L'Homme de Londre,* by Henri Decoin; *Les Caves du Majestic,* by Richard Pottier.

8. From 1930 to 1940, Jean Renoir directed: *On Purge Bébé, La Chienne, La Nuit du Carrefour, Chotard et Cie, Boudu Sauvé des Eaux, Madame Bovary, Toni, Le Crime de Monsieur Lange, La Vie Est à Nous, Une Partie de Campagne, Les Bas-Fonds, La Grande Illusion, La Marseillaise, La Bête Humaine, La Règle du Jeu.*

In the same decade, but after 1936, Marcel Carné directed: *Jenny, Drôle de Drame, Quai des Brumes, Hôtel du Nord, Le Jour Se Lève.*

9. From 1929 to 1940, Jacques Feyder directed: *Anna Christie* (1929), *Le Spectre Vert* (1930), *Si l'Empereur Savait Ça* (1930), *Le Fils du Radjah* (1931), *Le Grand Jeu* (1933), *Pension Mimosa* (1934), *La Kermesse Héroique* (1935), *Le Chevalier sans Armure* (1936), *Les Gens du Voyage* (1937), *La Loi du Nord* (1939). Feyder lived in Switzerland all during the Occupation.

For a Realistic Esthetic

Intellectuals are people who don't like to be interrupted. When the screen began to talk, they fell silent. It was not out of politeness. They like to convey the idea that it was rather out of contempt or disappointed love. We think it was out of resentment.

Agreed—such boorishness on the part of cinema was quite enough to vex our estheticians. So much bold thinking, so many stormy articles and discussions, such lavish advice, so many oracles without appeal—and all of it to lead to such ingratitude. In rejecting their rule, the cinema was abandoning itself to a low-grade realism. That was that—it would end badly.

The theoreticians and pedagogues of the Seventh Art were not completely wrong; nevertheless, we think that the absence of all effort at systematic thought in regard to the cinema for the last fifteen or twenty years is the sign of an abdication of responsibility, an abdication whose basic cause lies in an inability to understand the nature of cinema completely.

Cinema, like any naissant art, must be analyzed in its concrete complexity, in the totality of its relations with the social milieu apart from which it would not exist. Without prejudice to the idea of pure art, it can at least be emphasized that such an approach cannot be applied to popular arts charged by their very nature with functions foreign to esthetic laws. In our mechanized civilization, in which man is devoured by the technical aspects of his work and standardized by political and social restraints, the function of cinema, above even its artistic function, is to satisfy the immutable collective psychic needs that have been repressed. When these fundamental exigencies are finally clearly understood, criticism, working from these concrete *données,* will at last be able to attempt the elaboration of an esthetic that is simultaneously theoretical and practical—the only kind capable of explicating its object and having an effect on it. It is not our intention here to make a general judgment about the evolution of the other arts, about a painting, a poetry, a music, eager to eliminate all extrinsic elements in order to find in themselves the laws of their form. We merely say that to attempt the construction of a cinematic esthetic according to the same dialectic is a prime example of a false problem, because such a cinema will never come about. The cinema that will continue after we are gone will take into account the sociological, economic, and technical forces that determine it.

Are these forces intangible, incapable of being influenced? Are they by their nature incompatible with artistic demands? We will not venture an *a priori* reply, but we do know of at least some twenty silent and sound films, made within the framework of economic restraints or different politics, capable of proving that cinema, even operating within its social conditions, can rise to the level of great works of art.

Therefore, if we want to realistically and efficaciously think about the most significant esthetico-social development of modern times, if we want to eventually isolate the general laws of what the Seventh Art is and will be, we can do so only after first understanding its servitudes and functions. That is why, for example, the esthetician must study the psychology of the spectator's perception of the photographic image; understand, after research and statistical study, the reactions of the public to the different cinematic genres; discern, as a psychoanalyst of our civilization, the unconscious expectations of the millions of people whom the screen must sooner or later gratify; understand the role that cinema plays in contemporary politics, etc.

Only by building on these basic facts and understanding how they interact with the internal laws of cinematic expression will the esthetician be able to develop a synthesis of the Seventh Art.

The cinematic esthetic will be social, or cinema will have to do without an esthetic. (November 8, 1943)

Jean Delannoy's L'Eternel Retour

I hope that the delay—an involuntary one, actually—of this favorable review of *L'Eternel Retour* [1] will be correctly interpreted. Only cinematic works of this quality do not have to depend on the ephemeral interest aroused by their newness. A year from now we will be talking about *L'Eternel Retour,* just as we are still talking about *Les Visiteurs du Soir* without appearing ridiculous. Even such excellent films as *Le Corbeau* seem somewhat exhausted by the first bursts of criticism. It's not, of course, that anything is wrong with them, only that everything has been said about their qualities—or at least everything could have been said. All has not been said about Carné's film or about Delannoy's. [2]

To separate the woof from the warp, to sort out Cocteau's errors and Delannoy's merits, seems a very specious exercise to me. One might just as well continue the analysis until the director has been distinguished from the cameraman. Has this been done for Prévert and Laroche where *Les Visiteurs* is concerned? We don't know what Carné would be like without a good dialoguist, but *Adieu Léonard* has authoritatively demonstrated what happened to Prévert without Carné. Cocteau has generally been given the credit for that extraordinary character, the dwarf; but at the same time, what was heinous and unhealthy about the character was emphasized. As for me, if I were to congratulate anyone in particular on this point, it would more likely be the actor or the cameraman than the scenarist; I will explain why further on. Let us therefore end this pointless and somewhat prejudiced game of separating faults from merits and restore to the director the responsibility for the best and the worst.

Having said this, I must express the strongest reservations about the scenario, because implicit in it are all the weak-

L'Eternel Retour, a modern retelling of the Tristan story, starred Jean Marais and Madeleine Sologne. Bazin's enthusiasm for the film was tempered by his objections to Cocteau's script and its attempts at modern psychological causality. (Museum of Modern Art)

nesses of the film. In point of fact it was impossible to transcribe the novel about Tristan into a modern drama because the latter requires an internal verisimilitude of the characters and the action that myth can do without. The truth of legend is on a plane other than that of psychological realism; it is based on a spiritual symbolism and a metaphysical causality. Its power resides precisely in that often ambivalent generality of the symbol. The parables of the Bible can lend themselves to several exegeses and the Greek myths to many interpretations.

The direct projection of myth onto the plane of the psychological causality of modern realist drama is therefore a complete intellectual misapprehension. It results in the drama losing all verisimilitude and the symbol losing all prestige. For example, it is evident that the logic of the characters and situations requires that Patrice and Nathalie love each other upon their first encounter with the same love that will unite them after the formality of the philter-cocktail. We will pass over many other details in which respect for the legend led the action into the worst sort of absurdities. It results in a general uneasiness and a lack of credibil-

Despite the extraordinary acting of Piéral as the dwarf in Delannoy's *L'Eternel Retour* (1943), the expressive intensity shown here could not have been achieved without the lighting and angles of cameraman Roger Hubert. (Museum of Modern Art)

ity. I might add that the overall film design, subjected to the same servitude, so loses its rhythm and progression that this story of a cuckold drags a little. It is irritating to think of the extraordinary work that the art of Delannoy and his cameraman, Roger Hubert, might have given us if it had been in the service of a true tale of love.

That art surpasses anything that the French cinema has given us since the war—insofar as plastic expression is concerned. There are, of course, many reminders of *Les Visiteurs du Soir* in the film, but the style is so different that one cannot talk of plagiarism. It is not the fancifulness of the special effects that here creates the mystery, but the quality immanent in things and people, for which the cameraman can take almost all the credit. The shots of *Les Visiteurs* had a Mediterranean precision, all in black and white. Those of *L'Eternel Retour* give us a greater spiritual satisfaction because they incarnate the mystery and in some way make it perceptible in the grain of things.

I would have to analyze many images. The one, for example, in which we see united for the first time, in a close-up dolly shot, the faces of Patrice and Nathalie—a medallion engraved in the bronze of fate. The shots of the struggle with Moralt demonstrate an extraordinary sense of gesture and relief. Let us also cite the philter scene, with the discreetly employed innovation of the angle of vision of the characters lying on the ground, and finally the shot of the face and torso of the dead Patrice.

It should be said, moreover, that the quality of these images is not only dependent on the beauty of the photography—actually, beautiful photography can be the worst enemy of cinema—but on its expressive value and its dynamism; it is because of this that one cannot separate the director from the cameraman. If our first sight of the dwarf has so much dramatic power, it is because it has been prepared for at length by a dolly shot; and reciprocally, the face of the dwarf, despite the extraordinary acting of Piéral, would never have achieved that expressive intensity without the lighting and angles of Roger Hubert.

Actually, the personality of the actors is almost always effaced by the will of the director and the photographer, who treat them as sculptural material. Here, this is not simply a matter of technical skill but of the perfection of a style, with all that that word implies about spiritual content. This is so true that one suffers from not feeling the soul of the drama fill this magnificent body, which sometimes manages to create its own spirit.

With *L'Eternel Retour* we decidedly take another step on the road opened by *Les Visiteurs du Soir*. We no longer dare use the words "art film," because they evoke too many unhappy memories. However, an entire conception of the relations of cinema and poetry is defined by these works, though it is now no longer a question of borrowing untransmittable prestige from other arts, but of conquering an autonomous poetic language, in which Delannoy's film, after Carné's film, will mark a date in our cinematic history. In spite of its weaknesses, therefore, *L'Eternel Retour* marks an advance. Though more homogeneous, *Les Visiteurs du Soir* had not presented us with such perfect cinematic moments.

(November 20, 1943)

Notes

1. *L'Eternel Retour*: written by Jean Cocteau, directed by Jean Delannoy. Actors: Jean Marais, Madeleine Sologne, Jean Murat, Roland Toutain, Junie Astor, Piéral, Gabrielle Dorziat, Jean d'Yd, and Alexandre Rignault.

2. Jean Delannoy, who came to directing by way of editing, had directed *Paris-Deauville* (1935), *La Vénus de l'Or* (1937), *Le Diamant Noir* (1938), *Macao, l'Enfer du Jeu* (1940—this film was not authorized for release during the Occupation until Delannoy had reshot with Pierre Renoir all the scenes that had previously been done with Eric von Stroheim, whose anti-Nazism led him to Hollywood), *Fièvres* (1941), *L'Assassin A Peur la Nuit* (1942), and *Pontcarral* (1942). (F.T.)

Marcel Carné's Les Visiteurs du Soir
Robert Bresson's Les Anges du Péché

I may perhaps scandalize some readers by suggesting that of all French artistic activities the cinema is the only one to have made progress since the war. Understand me correctly; we have elsewhere known pleasures of the highest quality, but do they stand out as landmarks within a general progress? Could I speak of a renaissance of the novel, of painting, or of theater as I can—without being ridiculous—of the cinema?

This renaissance seems particularly paradoxical in that it applies to the art most heavily dependent on economic and social factors, an art destined by its very nature not for the delectation of intellectual elites but for the satisfaction of a popular public more than ever starved for escape and distraction, an art operating in the absence of our most famous directors, in the midst of the worst kinds of technical difficulties. Here is something that simultaneously testifies in favor of the much calumnied public and does honor to a pleiade of artists and technicians. Let us take advantage of the occasion to render unto Caesar the things which are Caesar's. It has not been made sufficiently clear that the Direction Générale du Cinéma, which has presided over the destinies of our screens since the war, has perhaps been somewhat responsible for this. In any case, let us note the coincidence and be sure that this official organization would inevitably have been blamed if we had to deplore a decline in the quality of production. As Marshall Joffre used to say of World War I: "I'm the one who would have lost it."

From *Les Visiteurs du Soir* to *L'Eternel Retour* by way of *Goupi Mains Rouges, Le Voyageur de la Toussaint, L'Honorable Catherine, Lumière d'Eté, Les Anges du Péché,* and *Le*

Corbeau—I'm omitting some, and good ones at that—the last cinematic season noticeably established the technical quality of our production. However, a distinction must be made between the simple technical skill to which we owe a good detective film and the intrinsic spiritual value of works. Now from this point of view, too, our cinema has put forth a considerable effort. I will therefore isolate from the season just over the three films that best represent the union between artistic mastery and indisputable spiritual quality. Obviously, the films I have in mind are *Les Visiteurs du Soir, L'Eternel Retour,* and *Les Anges du Péché.*

Les Visiteurs du Soir [1] exploded from the dreary production of 1941–1942 like a revolutionary event. It was immediately clear that it would mark a date, the beginning of an influence, the origin of a style. It had taken some courage on the part of the director, Marcel Carné, and the producer, A. Paulvé, to invest in this experiment four or five times the capital of an ordinary film. Initially, the public made them feel it. Indeed, the public doesn't like to have its habits disturbed, and the first to do this pay the cost. But with the help of snobbism, that happy snobbism that must sometimes be seen as a militant form of taste, *Les Visiteurs* little by little benefited from the swirl of opinion about it. Daily Homeric exchanges took place in the two first-run houses in Paris, while the provinces hesitated between stupor, enthusiasm, and rage; it even appears that several screens were bashed in. But *Les Visiteurs* won the day so completely that the diabolical, the fantastic, and the marvelous soon became the conventions of our present production.

Now that it is no longer necessary to defend it, we can speak of Carné's film with more impartiality. It is not absolutely a "great" film (let's say, so that we all know what we're talking about, that we apply that label to *La Grande Illusion*). To be that, it lacked a certain density, an epic elan, an authenticity, that warm—I was going to say charitable—sense of conviction which alone can really do the trick.

"*Les Visiteurs du Soir* exploded from the dreary production of 1941–1942 like a revolutionary event," Bazin wrote in 1943. Arletty, as one of the devil's envoys, kneels before Fernand Ledoux, the unsuspecting lord of the manor. (French Cultural Services)

The wit of dialoguists Prévert and Laroche partially made up for this, but the faith that goes with great creations cannot be replaced by skill and intelligence. Such as it is, this work nevertheless realizes a high poetic standard and, more generally, a spiritual one.

The theme is well known. Gilles and Dominique, two troubadours (one of whom is a woman in disguise), have signed a pact with the devil. They go from chateau to chateau

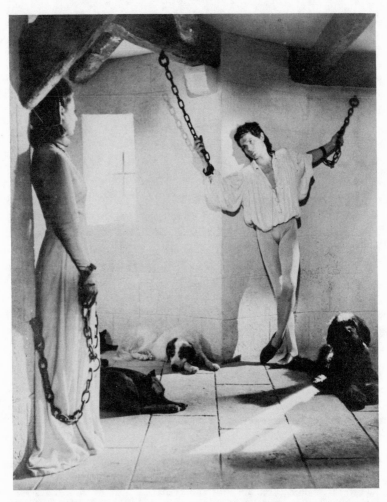

The invincible force of love will triumph over the supernatural wiles of Satan. Imprisoned because of their defiance are Anne (Marie Déa) and Gilles (Alain Cuny), a devil's envoy who refuses to play the devil's game. (Museum of Modern Art)

sowing the madness of the love which they inspire without sharing. In the chateau of Baron Hugue, the engagement of Anne, daughter of the lord, is being celebrated. The troubadours are admitted along with the acrobats and tumblers to participate in the celebration.

The enchantment is soon cast, and while Dominique seduces first the fiancé and then the baron, setting each against the other, Gilles makes Anne fall in love with him . . . But for the first time, ceasing to play the devil's game, he returns that love. From here on, the entire story is focused on the struggle of Satan, who has come in person to demand that the pact be carried out. But the supernatural force of the devil fails when faced with the invincible force of love, the essence of which neither suffering nor separation nor death can conquer. When, in despair, the devil changes the two lovers into statues, he is enraged to hear their hearts beating within the stone for all eternity. The debt of this subject to the romantic and courtly tradition of our medieval poetry is obvious, and it required considerable courage to present it to a popular audience in 1942.

But it is especially in the technique, or, more exactly, in the style, that the originality of the film asserts itself. Carné, completely turning away from the naturalist realism of *Quai des Brumes* and *Le Jour Se Lève,* tries for a poetry and an enchantment that are inherent in cinema. He is not always completely successful. The special effects and the double exposures sometimes lack the perfection necessary to their complete credibility; and in addition, the choice of Jules Berry and Marie Déa proved to be an awkward one. But these very failures are not lacking in intelligence, and the successes are high achievements. We will long remember the moment in which the ball is magically suspended so that Gilles and Dominique can step out of time to exercise their evil charms. We will also remember the spot of blood that clouds the water of the fountain in which Gilles and Anne are watching the tournament.

The director has used these methods discreetly, rejecting the easy way out offered by spectacular contrivances, fleeing the conventional, and having recourse to the marvelous only where its spiritual significance could be expressed in all its force. He has been magnificently seconded in his work by cameraman Roger Hubert, of whom we will speak again. For works of this class, the quality of the plastic expression is inseparable from the subject. The cameraman has here been able to create images in perfect harmony with the drama—sharp, black and white, spare and luminous like the Midi landscape that provides the background. This Provençal poem does not need the ambiguity of shadows to develop its spells. The mystery is completely contained in the souls of the beings and things that unflinchingly display their sun-scorched aspects.

I had always considered *Les Musiciens du Ciel*[2] as a paradoxical, almost miraculous, success—the dazzling exception to the rule that makes an artistic hell of French hagiographic or edifying cinema. It is not metaphysically impossible to make good cinema with "good" sentiments, but it must be recognized that the French creative temperament does not lend itself to it and that the epithet "good" has come to signify its contrary. The "good" film of the week—I mean, of course, "the parish week"—is too often one of which we should be wary out of principle.

Thanks to Father Bruckberger, to Giraudoux, and to Bresson we have a great film: *Les Anges du Péché*.[3] The combined talents of the scenarists, the dialoguist, the director, and the cameraman were none too many to avoid the multiple reefs and shoals of the subject. But the stereotypical is never so much as grazed. From the very first sequences we feel ourselves in good hands and we know that we will be brought to a safe harbor.

And yet the subject was fraught with danger: a novitiate with the rehabilitating Dominicans. A dramatic novitiate, because to conquer the soul of a rehabilitated "lost woman"—actually a backslider who has sought refuge in the convent after carrying out a crime of vengeance—the novice must come into conflict with the spiritual and human exigencies of the religious community. She must leave the convent

Directed by Robert Bresson from a script by Jean Giraudoux, *Les Anges du Péché* (1943) focused on a novice who finds herself in conflict with her religious community when a murderess seeks refuge in the convent. (French Cultural Services)

after an untimely outburst in the council; but no longer able to tolerate the idea of returning to the world she had abandoned, in despair at the thought that she had not been able to fulfill her mission to the one lost lamb, she wanders about the convent garden at night and in the morning is found sick, in a faint over a tomb. Before dying, she has the double joy of professing herself in the order and of converting, by her death, the one she had chosen above all others.

I don't know exactly what part Father Bruckberger played in the making of the film, nor in what measure he contributed to the scenario. One can, however, quite clearly distinguish what is undoubtedly due him: the exactitude. By that I mean not only the realism of the framework and the accuracy of the convent liturgy, but also the human truth, the psychological tissue of the life of the order in which the action takes place. The action itself suggests the influence of what might be called a technical adviser in matters of the spiritual life. There is no doubt that we owe much to his positive vigilance, from which Giraudoux brilliantly profited.

La Duchesse de Langeais had already given glimpses of the unexpected qualities as a cinematic dialoguist shown by the author of *Electre,* unexpected because it must be understood that the verbal exigencies of the screen are very different from those of the stage. However, *Les Anges du Péché* establishes, after the novelist and the playwright, a third Giraudoux, capable of renouncing all preciousness and of stripping his style to meet the elliptical demands of cinema. This dialogue, moreover, charms us no less by the elegance of its renunciations and its subtle sobriety than by our awareness of the perils it spares us.

If we had any reservations, they would perhaps derive from the very perfection of the dialogue. I mean that such a success is not achieved here without a certain departure—imperceptible—from authenticity. Giraudoux's text, though it cannot be criticized for any detail, betrays the fact that it is not the work of a believer. It is an elegant synthesis of the spiritual life from the point of view of a dazzling intelligence and talent, but it nevertheless remains a synthesis in that one area in which no artistic alchemy can replace the one thing necessary.

I have no space to expatiate as I should on the merits of Director Robert Bresson [4] and his cameraman Agostini. The actors are perfect (perhaps somewhat in the same way that M. Giraudoux is).

Les Anges du Péché is a film of stature, of "international stature." It demonstrates, along with *Les Visiteurs du Soir* and *L'Eternel Retour,* that the efforts of French cinema are not limited to those of a technical order but spill over into the intellectual and spiritual stance of our production.

(*Revue Jeux et Poésie*—end of 1943)

Notes

1. *Les Visiteurs du Soir.* Scenario: Pierre Laroche and Jacques Prévert. Photography: Roger Hubert. Sets: Wakhevitch and Trauner. Music: Maurice Thiriet and Joseph Kosma. Actors: Arletty, Marie Déa, Jules Berry, Fernand Ledoux, Alain Cuny, Marcel Herrand. (Grand Prix du Cinéma Français, 1942.)

2. Directed by Georges Lacombe, from a novel by René Lefevre (1939).

3. *Les Anges du Péché.* Direction: First feature film by Robert Bresson. Scenario: Father Bruckberger and Robert Bresson. Dialogue: Jean Giraudoux. Actors: Renée Faure, Jany Holt, Marie-Hélène Dasté, Yolande Laffon, Sylvia Montfort, Mila Parely, Louis Seigner. Cameraman: Philippe Agostini. Music: Jean-Jacques Grunewald. (Scenario published by N.R.F.: *Jean Giraudoux: Le Fils de Béthanie. Text of Les Anges du Péché.*)

4. *Les Anges du Péché* is the first feature-length film by Robert Bresson, who in 1934 had directed *Les Affaires Publiques,* a satirical medium-length film interpreted by the clown Babys. As co-scenarist or adaptor, Bresson had also worked on *Jumeaux de Brighton* (directed by Claude Heymann from a work by Tristan Bernard, 1936) and *Courrier Sud* (directed by Pierre Billon from a work by Saint-Exupéry, 1937). *Les Anges du Péché* was produced by Roland Tual, the maker of *Le Lit à Colonnes* (from the novel by Louise de Vilmorin) and, two years later, of *Bonsoir Mesdames, Bonsoir Messieurs,* the first and last scenario by Robert Desnos.

Pierre Blanchar's Un Seul Amour

A few words about Pierre Blanchar's new film: *Un Seul Amour.*[1] The subject of this romantic tale can be related in a few sentences. In order to marry the Vicomte de Clergues, Carla Biondi gives up dancing; she withdraws with her husband to the region of the Vendome. But the past is not to be so easily effaced. Carla Biondi realizes this when she is visited by one of her former lovers, who ignobly tries to blackmail her. Her husband suddenly appears. She hides her lover in a wall closet. A forgotten glove prevents the Vicomte de Clergues from being duped. He has the closet door bricked up, and then kills himself in an apparent hunting accident. A year later his wife rejoins him in death.

The names of Villiers de l'Isle-Adam, Nerval, and Edgar Allan Poe come to mind. Such an anecdote, excellent for a short story, seemed somewhat thin for a full-length film, so Bernard Zimmer resorted to the "flashback" technique—a technique that gave us Marcel Carné's admirable *Le Jour Se Lève,* but also André Valentin's *Marie-Martine* and André Berthomieu's *Le Secret de Madame Clapain,* to go back no further than that. To do this, Zimmer imagined that one of the Vicomte de Clergues' heirs had written a book, rather stupidly entitled *Un Seul Amour,* in which he told the story of the unblemished love that had all their lives united Carla Biondi and the Vicomte de Clergues. Now, just as he is about to approve the final proofs of his book, the naive author is brought evidence of his error. We then follow him as he seeks after this truth in which he does not want to believe and which he will decide to forget so that nothing in his book need be changed.

What results is a constant fragmentation of the action, which, though very skillfully handled, does not always seem to reinforce the dramatic power of the story. One gets the feeling that this principle could have been made use of in an infinitely more moving manner. It is also curious to note that an art which seems so readily to lend itself to this sort of "contrapuntal" technique of storytelling only utilizes it so rarely and so awkwardly.

We find in Pierre Blanchar's direction and in the film's overall continuity the qualities of *Secrets* [2]: the science of ellipsis and foreshortening, a supple linking of images, accompanied this time again by an indefinably naive and irritating quality. (We are specifically thinking of the dismaying naivete of the last shots, in which we see the soul of Micheline Presle rejoin that of Blanchar in the middle of a pasteboard garden awash in elegiac mists.)

Piménoff's sets do not always allow us to forget the fibrocement and stucco of which they are made.

Arthur Honegger's musical score is not commonplace, but a little emphatic.

In short, a quality film that can be seen with pleasure but that takes its place in the norm of French production with a much too visible complacency! (December 4, 1943)

Notes

1. *Un Seul Amour*. Direction: Pierre Blanchar. Adaptation: Bernard Zimmer from a story by Balzac, "La Grande Bretèche." Photography: Christian Matras. Actors: Pierre Blanchar, Micheline Presle.
2. *Secrets* (1942), Pierre Blanchar's first directorial assignment in the cinema, was adapted from Turgeniev's play *A Month in the Country*.

Toward a Cinematic Criticism

It's not that we naively attach more importance than we should to the effectiveness of film criticism. The opinions of several unhappy journalists do not yet weigh much in the balance against the prestige of Fernandel. Exhibitors are interested only in the previous box-office receipts, and the public only in the names of the stars. The cinematic press is read only by a minority of filmgoers—mostly Parisians. The film market is still controlled by laws of social psychology similar to those that before the war influenced the sale of printed matter. It is generally agreed that these laws are not solely esthetic.

Does that mean that criticism could disappear without any loss? On the contrary, we believe it indispensable to the development and future of the cinema. Because it is not, like the other arts, aimed at an elite but at several million passive spectators in search of a couple of hours of escape, the cinema cannot realistically be controlled by anything other than production. The free play of sociological forces and economic factors at the point of purchase inevitably establishes the average film at a certain collective mental level which it would be interesting to describe. It is not our intention in saying this to express contempt for a public from which we do not separate ourselves, but which, because of its number, partakes of mass psychology.

The public will always prefer—if one respects certain psychological conditions—a good film to a bad one; by this we simply mean that the quality of films cannot be modified by first educating the taste of the public, but that on the contrary it is necessary to first modify the quality of films so that they can educate the public. Everything we know about the social restrictions under which cinema operates proves that though the other arts are inconceivable without esthetic liberalism, cinema is absolutely incapable of existing without managerial direction. Indeed, the conditions that allow it to live are not yet those of an art but simply of an image-industry under a liberal capitalist regime. Since it is not our object to study the possible modalities of an esthetic control of production, we will limit ourselves to the film itself; the dialoguists and scenarists are for the most part writers who went to work for the cinema. They belong to the same literary milieu. Alexandre Arnoux, for example, is simultaneously a scenarist and a critic.[1] The thermometer of box-office receipts has its importance, but the opinion of the

Café de Flore will not be negligible as long as cinematic creation remains partly in the hands of intellectuals.

Let us begin by distinguishing—we will return to this point—between oral criticism and written criticism. The first is, in any case, more effective than the second because it is more competent, more abundant, tougher and more sincere; but the one cannot do without the other. The press assures a certain flurry of notoriety to the judgments that competent circles have made about a film. These debates must not take place behind closed doors. If the public too often gets only a travesty of judgment, it is because of the incompetence or dishonesty of the journalist; but that is another story.

The direct influence of criticism on cinematic production thus strikes us as definite, though still limited. Let us turn now to the movie theaters and ask to what extent the customers also have become more demanding about quality. We have just expressed our pessimism about the influence of criticism on the public. It is true that this influence is still weak and without proportion to its object, but we can see that it is slowly increasing. Certain film columns are attracting increased readership, and their authority is becoming established. Little by little there is being created an elite of film-lovers capable of judging what is offered them. I need only point out the example of the swirl of opinion about *Les Visiteurs du Soir*. The reader of the weekly publication or journal is becoming accustomed to seeing the same typographic importance given to accounts of both the theater and the movies—the latter reviews provided, moreover, by a novelist or a musician, or a political writer or a dramatist, or even a poet.

The days are long since past when Paul Souday could tell a *Nouvelles Littéraires* interviewer that a serious critic could not concern himself with the cinema. We already have a history of the Seventh Art by a Sorbonne professor, and one day we will have an 800-page thesis on the comic art of American cinema between 1905 and 1917 or something like that. And who then would dare maintain that the subject cannot be taken seriously?

Thanks to the formation of this elite, cinema is little by little ceasing to be a secret alchemy of a few knowledgeable technicians, something offered to millions of faithful and ignorant spectators. There is slowly being formed the vital conditions necessary to all art: no art, not even a popular one, can do without an elite.

All very well, the reader will say, but where is this criticism? We willingly acknowledge our abuse of the present indicative. It was, alas, only a working hypothesis. How many critics really do their jobs? So as not to flatter anyone, we will not give our estimate of the number but will merely tell the reader that it is up to him to demand such criticism. Though several thousand enlightened film-lovers are powerless against a production destined for several million customers, perhaps they may be able to do something about the specialized press. The weeklies and the journals are addressed to a relatively limited public. Literary and artistic columns play a role in the economy of these publications. Reactions that cannot pragmatically be asked of the anonymous masses in the movie theaters can perhaps be expected of the reader of *Comoedia*. In the name of certain basic principles, we would like to see some precise demands made on a criticism that is at present inadequate, incompetent, or insincere. It is this that we will attempt to do in a criticism of criticism.

First let us recognize that the movie columnist is in a very different situation from that of his colleagues, who have inherited a long tradition and have a public of well-defined readers. The historical and sociological conditions under which the cinema operates make it vitally important for the movies to address themselves to all publics simultaneously—

from the concierge to the novelist; but the concierge reads only [publications which tell the "story," such as] *Le Film Complet* and collects photos of stars; she couldn't care less about M. Audiberti.[2] We are confronted by an art that is popular and a criticism that is not, and face the temptation of raising that art to the social and intellectual level of its criticism. Because intellectual musicians, painters, poets, and estheticians of all sorts were interested in cinema, they wanted to subject it to laws that were foreign to it, to make of it, like their poetry or their painting, an art for initiates. Anybody who leafs through cinematic publications from 1924 to 1930 will be able to understand this point.

Because the new economic restraints created by sound films rapidly cleared the terrain, these publications barely survived silent films, but the essence of these restraints was already present within the silent cinema. Any elite esthetic is radically incompatible with the basic laws of cinema. Cinema has need of an elite, but that elite will be influential only to the extent that it realistically understands the sociological demands of the Seventh Art. The only way to serve it effectively is to discover under what conditions a film destined for several million spectators interested above all in escape can nevertheless be an art. These conditions do exist, as is proved by the fact that certain films have realized them. It is up to the critic to define them and bring his opinions into line with them.

Let nobody say that all tastes have to be provided for in a field in which, alas, we are well below any taste. The truth is, on the contrary, that the crisis of cinema is less of an esthetic than an intellectual order. What film production basically suffers from is stupidity, a stupidity so overwhelming that esthetic quarrels are relegated to a secondary level. This is no longer a value judgment but a question of positive evidence. If our cinematic output were well-balanced, it would have been possible to argue before the public the merits of *Les Visiteurs du Soir*; however, faced with the stupidity of *Le Voile Bleu* [3] or *Patricia,*[4] it wasn't possible to do anything but fiercely defend that oasis of intelligence and honest technique.

We will not only ask of the critic that in his way he be a sociologist of art, but also that he have a minimal technical competence. Oh, not that he has tried making movies himself—his colleagues don't necessarily have a play or an opera to their credit, but at least they know what they are talking about. They can recognize a badly constructed play or an error in harmony. They have read or heard their classics. After all, they know syntax and can read music. But one sometimes angrily wonders if those who undertake to write of the cinema have even an elementary notion of its means of expression, because if they do, they give no hint of it.

Can one imagine an opera critic who criticizes only the libretto? Yet where most of our film reviews are concerned, it is useless to look for an opinion about the decor or the quality of the photography, for judgments on the use of sound, for details on the continuity—in a word, for that which constitutes cinema. If these basics were not lost sight of, nine times out of ten we would have critical unanimity at least about the workmanship of a film. Because what is true of stupidity is also true of film—below a certain level no discussion is possible.

Now we don't ask all that much of a film before qualifying it as "good." We ask that it not be stupid and that it be skillfully shot by making opportune use of the means of expression proper to the cinema. The first judgment is intellectual—we have said what we think of that—and the second is technical. After all, two carpenters would agree about the solidity of a table, and we don't really see why our critics, if they knew their profession, couldn't also agree about perfectly objective facts. Such facts would, of course, not be enough to evaluate a film like *La Grande Illusion, Quai des Brumes, Les Visiteurs du Soir,* or *L'Eternel Retour,* because in those cases what it necessary is an esthetic judgment on the style of a work. But I don't forbid my critic to make such judgments—I merely doubt his authority when he has been unable to condemn as he should, for its stupidity and bad workmanship, this week's hit. An indisputable competence in other domains is, therefore, not license enough to write impressionistic criticism of the Seventh Art, no matter how witty and amusing this criticism may be to read. We want a little more respect, first for the cinema and then for the reader.

This reader of the literary weekly generally has at least a minimum of culture. It is impossible to conceive of a drama column written as though the history of theater since Aeschylus simply didn't exist. We don't ask of weekly criticism that it be a comparative history of cinema, we ask only that the critic not be unaware of this history and not limit it to the current season. Our decadence is surely in part due to this singular faculty of forgetfulness. If nobody had read Molière after his death, what would be the use of Molière? This is the very principle of any esthetic that is to be judged. There is no art that is not supported by a culture, and there is no culture without historical judgment. No doubt where cinema is concerned, we are faced with an art whose past productions are still for all practical purposes inaccessible; but this is only another reason for criticism to make every effort to assume the responsibility for the cinematic culture of its readers. As it happens, more than one of these readers has witnessed the development of cinema; in the absence of documents, he would need only to have his memory refreshed. Cinema already has its primitives and its classics, but where most criticism is concerned, it is useless to look for an allusion to this history, for a rapprochement in time or in space, for the recognition of an influence. One would think that, like the intangible shadows on the screen, this unusual art has no past, leaves no traces, has no depth. It is more than time to invent a criticism in relief.

A little bit of historical perspective would also help put some order into the present confusion of a criticism lacking fixed references. The different Paris theaters practically specialize in certain dramatic genres. Their regular publics know more or less what they will find there. The Grand Guignol and L'Ambigu theaters don't offer the repertory of the Comédie Française. The reader of a review of [Henry de Montherlant's] *La Reine Morte* or of [Jean-Paul Sartre's] *Les Mouches* has a pretty good idea of the esthetic level of these plays and knows that they are very different from the comedies at the Palais-Royal.

Nobody would ever think of comparing the merits of a boulevard comedy with those of [Jean Giraudoux's] *La Guerre de Troie N'aura pas Lieu*. Because the cinema does not have specialized theaters or publics, because films necessarily address themselves to the entire public, cinematic works are treated as though they too did not have their genres and their hierarchies. As a result, films that have nothing in common have similar labels applied to them. *Goupi Mains Rouges* is an almost perfect work, whereas *Les Visiteurs du Soir* has weaknesses, but the genre to which Becker's film belongs is esthetically inferior to that of Carné's film. Judgments only make sense within the same genre, within a related style. The first hierarchy must therefore initially be established among the genres themselves. There are important films that do not succeed completely, and there are amusing little stories that are completely successful. We blush to have to formulate such truisms. It is, alas, necessary to do so.

Because they have to report on minor works, some critics have become accustomed to finding unsuspected charms in them. In this universe without grandeur, simple honesty has assumed the proportions of genius in their eyes. When they come across real grandeur, however, they run out of steam and are completely happy and content, after that momentary flood, to get back to the reassuring level of weekly production.

Criticism respectful of its art should not lose sight of certain scales of value and should cling to them, perhaps ascending to higher echelons only two or three times a year. But they would have to cling to their severity with a little more perseverance.

Now, many of our critics are afraid of being severe, and when they cease to be severe they simultaneously cease to be just. Dare we ask why? Dare we remind them that the golden rule of all criticism is independence, that a judge sensible to arguments other than those of justice (a justice that can be militant) is guilty of a breach of duty? This is not the place to open the debate about the servitudes French criticism is subject to, but perhaps someday that will have to be done. Let's merely say that a journalist—competent and resolved to write every week exactly what he thinks of the new films—will surely not find many publications ready to print him. A good number of prewar serious critics have therefore given up the struggle and ceded their place to inoffensive and amusing chroniclers.

We are ashamed to have to remind readers of such basic verities, because at bottom we ask nothing more than what is naturally expected of all other criticism: a minimum of intelligence, of culture, and of honesty. But isn't this simply to remind readers that cinema is an art, if only potentially? Though they occasionally proclaim this, some critics feel free to treat it as though it weren't, and they no longer respect the basic laws of criticism. Do they really think they are helping cinema with this philandering or with this somewhat condescending insiders' complicity which presides over the witty reports, the poetic observations, or the kind of accounts of what's going on around town that takes the place of cinematic criticism in a would-be literary press?

We fully understand, however, that this criticism is subject to exigencies that do not apply to the other arts—at least to the same degree. This is because of the topicality of the cinematic work, which is unavoidably ephemeral given present-day marketing procedures. But this topicality should have a beneficial influence on criticism by emphasizing its militant character. Those who unreservedly praised *Les Visiteurs du Soir* have done their duty because they completely supported a work for which the present condition of French cinema obliged complete support. A film should not only be judged on its absolute value but for the effort that it represents under given production conditions, and for the progress in that production that it makes possible. That is why snobbism must be utilized by the critic.

There is no longer any need to make an apologia for snobbism. In the modern corporate world, snobbism is initially the patronage of imbeciles. Since the mass of these unconscious Maecenas have no reasons for their opinions, the problem becomes one of an effective politic of snobbism within the more general framework of a politic of cinema. It would be childish to accuse us of esthetic Machiavelianism when all we are proposing is that we fight with arms—which are in the final analysis intellectually superior—that other, lower-grade snobbism: the depraved cult of the star. In any case, we would have no trouble finding in the history of the relations between art and fashion a reasonable justification of our proposition: in its own time, Romanticism was also a snobbism.

Now this politic must be directed by an intelligent criticism aware of its responsibilities, just as, for once, it understood them where *Les Visiteurs du Soir* was concerned. Without such a politic, Carné's film would not have taken on the bellicose allure of a manifesto. Let us, however, say that the public should not only be beguiled in favor of such a good film but also led to reject bad films. It's all very well to endorse the opinion that the unreserved admiration of *Les Visiteurs du Soir* is a diploma of intelligence and good taste, but it is also necessary to see to it that every filmgoer imbued with intelligence and a claim to good taste will be ashamed to go and shed a tear over [novelist] Henri Bordeaux's latest filmed melodrama. We still haven't managed that. A battle of *Les Visiteurs du Soir* is all very well, but we need a generalized civil war.

The point is that snobbism—and this will be the second point in our apologia—is not only the patronage of imbeciles; it is also, where intelligent people are concerned, what is currently necessary in the esthetic war. Snobbism is a militant form of taste. People don't fight without prejudice or passion; they reserve their anxiety about not being taken in for private moments. *Les Visiteurs du Soir* is decidedly a significant example of this. Almost all the specialists are of the opinion that this film has many faults. It is a film that doesn't achieve its ambitions. The oral criticism of which I spoke previously was extremely severe on this point, and yet it was necessary that published accounts be unanimous. From the militant and historical point of view, this film had to be unreservedly praised because it represented the greatest effort of European cinema since the war to raise the Seventh Art to an authentic poetry.

Criticism must seize the exceptional opportunity offered by the temporary disappearance of movie magazines specializing in the cult of the star to assume responsibility for this worthwhile fight.

The establishment of a certain specialization of criticism is also desirable. The daily press could provide a synopsis of the film and give a succinct opinion about its technical and artistic merits. In delivering this opinion it could make known the director, the dialoguist, etc. . . . , recalling as necessary their previous works. Even as it supplies what the popular public expects above all—an account of the plot—it would work to gain acceptance for the idea that a film's worth stems from its auteurs and that it is much safer to put one's faith in the director than in the leading man. The attention that the man in the street gives to the composition of a soccer team—the competence, the discrimination, the memory for detail, the kind of erudition he shows when what is involved is a sport which is for him basically only a spectacle —why wouldn't he be capable of all this when what is involved is an art that he feeds on weekly and that has an extraordinary place in his leisure and dreams? Cinema is a team sport in which each man makes his contribution toward winning the game, and that contribution is not so mysterious. The mechanic can as easily understand the role of a cameraman as he can the contribution of the left wing player. It need only be explained to him. All that is necessary is to make him understand that it is impossible to know anything about the cinema without being aware of a certain number of names, which are not necessarily those of the actors. It should be easy, by appealing to the popular taste for expertise, to create in opposition to the cult of the star a counter-snobbism of the technician. In this way we will see develop a healthy written popularization of cinema, which will, however, be no less popular than the biography of Danielle Darrieux.

In the weekly literary press, criticism—addressing itself to a more limited public—would no longer aim only for popularization but also for a true cinematic culture. This kind of criticism has been our particular concern in this article. However, we should not lose sight of the fact that the readership of the weeklies is not always accustomed to find in film accounts the same information it finds in other articles. Sacrifices will have to be made to current importance, mundanity, and style. There is something even sadder than a bad critic—criticism which isn't read.

But let's not exaggerate; we are very aware that the most widely read film columnists today are also the most competent and the most sincere. This criticism which appears in the weekly press is important: it is the criticism that can recruit a cultivated public for the cinema; it is the criticism that creates movements of opinion. That is why it must be strongly militant; that is also why its lack of rigor strikes us as a betrayal, a squandering of a wonderful opportunity.

Finally, we would see a third class of criticism—criticism in journals no longer aimed at the average man but at the knowledgeable film-lover; addressing itself to connoisseurs, it would by definition no longer have to sacrifice to snobbism. Without ceasing to be militant, this criticism could exactly reflect the oral criticism mentioned above. Comparable on all points to literary, musical, or art criticism, it would cede nothing to them in terms of technical and historical erudition. It is even possible to imagine specialized cinematic publications that would be to the Seventh Art what other so-called "serious" publications are to painting or music.

To those who find such a demand utopian and exaggeratedly severe, we will simply say: "We have asked for nothing, described nothing, desired nothing, that the silent cinema and the beginning of sound films had not already abundantly known. The fact that in ten years this cinematic press could have been so forgotten only proves that the decadence of almost all our criticism perhaps makes it necessary to recall these few basic truths."   (December 11, 1943)

Notes

1. Alexandre Arnoux, a member of the Académie Goncourt, wrote for *Mercure de France, Le Figaro, Nouvelles Littéraires.* He was also editor in chief of *Pour Vous.* As a dialoguist he contributed to Jacques Feyder's *La Loi du Nord* (1939) and Louis Daquin's *Premier de Cordée* (1943). (F.T.)

2. Jacques Audiberti did the film column of the weekly *Comoedia.*

3. This melodrama by Jean Stelli (1943), from a scenario by François Campeaux, broke all box-office records for the year 1942. (F.T.)

4. *Patricia,* directed by Paul Mesnier from a story by Clément Vautel.

Jean Grémillon's Le Ciel Est à Vous

If you have any doubts about the usefulness of cinematic criticism, think of *Le Ciel Est à Vous*.[1] This unpublicized and star-less film would certainly have gone unnoticed by the public if it had not been for the vigilance of a few journalists. Since it had none of the usual attractions working for it, it would perhaps have gone the way of the ordinary little melodrama. Thanks to a team of columnists, *Le Ciel Est à Vous* has already created as much controversy as *Les Visiteurs du Soir*.

However, now that the success of Grémillon's film is assured, it is permissible to nuance that praise a bit without feeling remorse. In spite of its astonishing qualities, it is not true that this work is perfect. The scenario, despite the style, about which we will have more to say later, is not always free of a slight childishness. The same subject could have been treated with more vigor. Just a bit of tartness, as psychological counterpoint, would have given the drama a tension it sometimes lacks. And to get all these reservations out of the way once and for all, let us also say that it was wrong to give equal praise to the entire cast.

Madeleine Renaud and Debucourt are clearly not up to the others. They are both too intelligent as artists. The simplicity Grémillon has imposed on them forces them to make compromises in the way they play the characters. Where Madeleine Renaud—always dazzling when given roles that are witty, nuanced, and delicate—is concerned, the casting error was particularly noticeable. Needless to say she manages her role as an honest workingman's wife, but she plays it too much like a member of the Comédie Française, whereas the little-known faces of the other actors have a poignant authenticity. The amazing creation of Charles Vanel cannot be praised too highly. This artist's career is relaunched. We knew he was a good actor, but here he is one of international stature. Only the best performances of Raimu sometimes achieve as much power and truth.

But the originality of this film resides principally in the amazing relationship of form and content. It would have been hard to dream up more unusual situations, to make more frequent use of the sentimental conventions of the *Veillée des Chaumières*—to say nothing of *La Bibliothèque Rose*. Nevertheless, this scenario that might have been drawn from a serial in a ladies' fashion magazine was actually based on a true incident, and the miracle of Grémillon's art was to restore situations shopworn by the literature of edification or melodrama to the virginity of a documentary—to a heart-breaking precision, believability, and realism. It is not the tears shed that prove the worth of a drama. What is important is their spiritual salt. Margot will weep as she did at the previous week's melodrama, but she will be aware that her tears do not have the same taste, that they have the salt of truth.

It required unusual skill to disclose under the counterfeit of the stereotype the original source in reality itself. Grémillon's art is worthy of long commentaries.[2] This director, who had given us proof of his cinematic virtuosity in *Lumière d'Eté,* here achieves, thanks to his mastery, an extraordinary effacement of technique. He expresses himself in a visual prose of an honesty and transparency so perfect that we cease to be aware of technique. At this degree of skill, art completely disappears into its object; we are no longer at the cinema but in life itself. It could be said of this cinematic language that it achieves what Gide, Martin du Gard, and Alain preach as the supreme quality of novelistic prose—the complete banality of style. As a result, *Le Ciel Est à Vous* is one of the rare French films since Jean Renoir's *Le Crime de Monsieur Lange,* to support comparison with the contemporary novel. (February 26, 1944)

Notes

1. *Le Ciel Est à Vous.* Direction: Jean Grémillon. Scenario: Albert Valentin and Charles Spaak. Photography: Louis Page. Sets: Max Douy. Music: Roland-Manuel. Actors: Madeleine Renaud, Charles Vanel, Jean Debucourt, Léonce Corne, Albert Rémy, Michel François.

2. Since the introduction of sound films, Jean Grémillon has directed *La Petite Lise* (1930), *Dainah la Métisse* (1931), *Pour un Sou d'Amour* (1932), *La Dolorosa* (1934), *Centinella Alerta* (1935), *La Valse Royale* (1935), *Pattes de Mouches* (1936), *Gueule d'Amour* (1937), *L'Etrange Monsieur Victor* (1938), *Remorques* (1939–41), *Lumière d'Eté* (1942).

To Create a Public

On Sunday, February 27th and on the following Sunday, March 5th, there were two special preformances during which Jean Grèmillon and Raoul Ploquin came to present *Le Ciel Est à Vous,* and Louis Daquin to present *Premier de Cordée.*[1] These sessions, organized in collaboration with the Service des Etudiants by the Institute des Hautes Etudes Cinématographiques (IDHEC), are part of a program for which the young Université du Cinéma originally turned to the very ancient Université de Paris.

When the idea of a cinema study group was proposed in a student center less than two years ago, this initiative was not taken very seriously, and the two leaders had a great deal of difficulty in recruiting a third adherent. Times have changed. Last week the student ticket bureau on rue Soufflot had to post a notice—like the neighboring tobacco counter that had run out of matches—that there were no more tickets for *Premier de Cordée.* Hundreds of students were unable to attend these two showings, which took place in theaters filled to the bursting point. In all the student centers, cinema groups are being set up; groups are being formed in several lycées and universities. There seems to be a general university movement in favor of cinema.

Every effort aimed at forming an enlightened cinema public capable of reacting and judging adds a stone to the overall creation itself. A school for film technicians is not possible without a school for spectators. The turnouts of these two recent Sundays are therefore a response to the desire to establish active relations between the work and the public.

Cinema has often been reproached for the passivity of its public, which is simultaneously individualistic and gregarious; this passivity has been contrasted with the communal response of a theater audience—an audience dominated by the chandelier, that luminous, crystalline, circular, and symmetrical object so dear to Baudelaire—to the performance of actors. The cinema knows only indirect lighting and the long prism of rigid light—the agile comet or the ray of moonlight from the projectionist's booth—which carries within it only shadow and fugitive illusions. It was therefore interesting to create in a movie house a community of spectators, a homogeneous public that felt itself at one with the work. Before the community of this public could really crystallize, it was also necessary that the work no longer be only a disembodied image but that it rediscover something of that human "presence" of the theater. This is why the authors, directors, and producers came in person to present their films. As a result, very naturally and without ridiculousness, the customary expression of the theatrical community found a place here: I mean, of course, applause.

The significance of this human ambiance was strongly felt by the students, but it was no less sensed by the makers of the films. Daquin is fond of saying that the director has insufficient contact with the public, that moreover, practically speaking, the cinematic auteur cannot intellectually break out of professional circles—that he lacks points of reference, real information about the needs and the expectations of the public, which is known only through the pressure gauge of box-office receipts. All direct human testimony, therefore, provides the film creator with precious information.

But such turnouts acquire their complete sense only if the students attend them regularly and if they are concerned with making a critical effort. In his short speech last Sunday, M. Gérin, head of IDHEC, declared: "This direct contact between spectators and filmmakers imposes a duty on you: the duty of further deepening, from film showing to film showing, your cinematic culture so that your testimony is truer, deeper, and more useful to the art of film."

I would not like to conclude this article without congratulating Raoul Ploquin, Pathé, and *L'Ecran Français* for the understanding they as producers showed of this formula, because it was like a little revolution in the mores of cinematic exploitation. There are ticket buyers who may perhaps have failed to understand that an apparently exact multiplication can be false in spite of the fact that it has been proved by casting out the nines.   (March 18, 1944)

Notes

1. *Premier de Cordée*. Direction by Louis Daquin from a novel by Frison Roche; adaptation and dialogue by Alexandre Arnoux. Actors: André Le Gall, Jean Davy, Irène Corday, Mona Doll, Maurice Baquet, Roger Blin.

On Realism

It is the mechanical genesis of photography that makes its specific properties different from those of painting. For the first time the realism of the image achieved entire objectivity and made of the photograph a sort of ontological equivalent of the model. (Because of this, the human body, a privileged object in all the plastic arts, is almost inevitably obscene or pornographic on the screen.) Let us, however, begin by distinguishing the technical "realism" of the image from the "realism" of the plastic or dramatic content. Thus *Les Visiteurs du Soir* is no less "realistic" in the first sense of the word than *Le Corbeau,* since both these works are cast in the objectivity of photographic matter; but the marvelous and the fantastic of Carné's film is in opposition to the "realistic" observation of Clouzot's.

Technical "realism" is thus at the very heart of cinema. It may constitute its essence. It could also constitute its weakness.

All arts that have a temporal factor imply an incessant re-creation of the work around a permanent nucleus, literary or musical. Each evening a play is reborn anew from its text in front of the footlights. Its eternity is inseparable from the current living "presence" of the execution. There have been and will be as many *Phèdres* as there are performances of the tragedy. The dramatic work includes both a soma and a germen. This is the price it pays for being itself. In other words, if the only *Phèdre* we had was a sound film of its first performance, Jean Racine would no longer exist.

The point is that film necessarily fixes the work of art in a certain historical and social context (as a matter of fact, the last photographic bath is called a "fixer"). It is not only the objects, the costumes, the makeup, the thousand details dating the space around man that limit our participation in the drama; it is man himself, interpreting his society through the least of his gestures, his way of walking or smiling. The symphony or the tragedy follows us from our childhood to our old age; its eternity is always contemporary with us. Film, on the contrary, remains by its very nature anchored in the moment of its birth. What is conserved in the layer of film gelatin is only fossilized time.

Here the two realisms, technical and esthetic, meet and determine each other. It might be thought that all that need be done to cast off temporal servitude is to get rid of its most obvious signs in costuming or action, to choose a medieval or classical subject, to deal with dreams and unreality.

Alas, this notion couldn't be further from the truth, since man himself, even nude, is sufficient to express the entire society. Besides, nothing is more revealing of an epoch than the choice and style of its escapism. There is no doubt, for example, that whatever the esthetic value and interest of *Les Visiteurs du Soir* and *L'Eternel Retour,* these works will surely age.

Why, on the contrary, does the least Max Linder film (see an early Lumière Brothers reel)—so marked by all the details of decor, so precisely localized in time and social space —completely escape aging? Why after fifteen years does a work like Murnau's *Tabu* strike us as being as fresh as a young virgin of the isles? For reasons which are basically identical: both are saved by their submission to realism. Cinema cannot escape its essence. It can achieve the eternal only by unreservedly searching for it in the exactitude of the instant. *Tabu* has not aged because it remains basically a documentary—in other words, pure observation and realism. Max Linder continues to touch us because his human message is expressed in genres that were always essentially realistic: comedy and farce. And here one might wonder if certain Molière farces could not have been transmitted to us on film without loss, although a similar sound film of *Phèdre* remains inconceivable.

Cinema can, therefore, also work for eternity. But such works, here as in the other arts, can only be born from intimate congruity with physical laws and with the psychological structure of cinematic matter. The objective realism of the camera irrevocably determines its esthetic.   (April 15, 1944)

The Art of Not Seeing Films

The lean kine succeed one another. I am speaking, alas, figuratively. During the last two weeks, I have been unable to bring myself to go to the movies. Between *La Collection Ménard* [1] and *Le Bal des Passants*,[2] there is unfortunately little to choose.

Last year, along with several friends from the cinema group of the Maison des Lettres, I had seen the filming of a shot from *La Collection Ménard* at the François Premier studio. Just one—and not a very significant one—but the entire style of the film was implicit in this wretched shot: the vulgarity of the dialogue, the stupidity of the scenario, the lack of conviction on the part of the actors who had embarked on this commercial galley. So true is it that most films can be judged by very slight elements—sometimes by their titles (though there is *Les Anges du Péché*) and almost always by a simple still—that the criticism we had made *a priori* coincides exactly with what is now being said about the film by "the" competent columnists.

A rapid examination of the advertising still outside a movie makes it possible to eliminate many films from consideration. A bad film can almost always be spotted by using this criterion alone. About 75 percent of film production could be judged without appeal this way. Try it. It requires less application than graphology. A basic characterological study of the film showing in your neighborhood theater requires only a little judgment and psychology.

The actual technical quality of the photography provides a first indication. One can use as a point of departure the principle that idiocy is homogeneous (I naturally except Abel Gance, a dazzling proof of the rule). A good photograph is also an intelligent photograph. At least it assures that even if the film is bad, it will not sink into silliness. This was, for example, true of Serge de Poligny's *Le Baron Fantôme*.[3]

The actors are another indication. Beware of the multiplicity of stars; it almost always reveals the poverty of the scenario. The conjunctions of Raimus, Fernandels, Michel Simons, Jules Berrys, Jean Tissiers, etc., is *a priori* a bad sign. Of course, from time to time there is a *Carnet de Bal*. But don't worry; the news about it spreads fairly quickly. Also examine closely what the characters look like. Here too psychological falseness and stupidity are linked. It's easy to spot if the actors have adopted sentimental stereotypes or, what is worse, the stereotype of their character as star. The decor too provides information about the taste and honesty of the director, about the style of the film. The pointlessly sumptuous salons, the bedrooms as big as railway stations, the double-winged marble stairways, often reveal, along with other signs, the esthetic demagogy, the inflation of what are intended to be external signs of beauty.

Eventually you will distinguish even more subtle elements. With some film-going experience, you will sense just which family of flop the film whose still you are analyzing belongs to. Naturally, a little intuition doesn't hurt. This cluster of basic observations, along with information about the credits and the reading of one or two carefully chosen critics, will allow you 75 percent of the time to choose with certainty. There will be disappointments enough in the other 25 percent, but at least you will be spared losing your time with films that are no more worthy of comment than your grocer's picture calendars or bathing beach chromos are worthy of comparison with what is merely an ordinarily honest painting. (May 6, 1944)

Notes

1. Directed by Bernard Roland from a scenario by Jacques Viot.
2. Directed by Guillaume Radot.
3. *Le Baron Fantôme* (1942). Director: Serge de Poligny. Scenario: Serge de Poligny. Adaptation: Serge de Poligny and Louis Chavance. Dialogue: Jean Cocteau. Actors: Alain Cuny, André Lefaur, Alerme, Aimé Clariond, Claude Sainval, Marcel Perez, Jany Holt, Odette Joyeux, Gabrielle Dorziat, and, in the role of the phantom, Jean Cocteau himself.

Marcel L'Herbier's La Nuit Fantastique

The Institut des Hautes Etudes Cinématographiques [1] and the Service des Etudiants, which had been obliged because of electricity cuts to suspend the series of showings reserved for students, were able, thanks to M. André Robert and the Union Technique Cinématographique to resume their sessions by presenting on Sunday, May 7th, Marcel L'Herbier's *La Nuit Fantastique.* [2]

The director himself presented the film in a short but brilliant talk in which he took to task the unfortunately too widespread anti-artistic mores of certain film distributors and theater managers. We can remember the helpless rage that sometimes gripped us in provincial movie theaters, where we were coolly presented with a film from which a reel had been amputated. In defense of the manager interested in fitting two feature films into his program, it might be claimed that the public would never notice. It could have been shown the reels in reverse order without raising a protest. But the passivity of the public is no excuse; respect for the consumer should be the first moral principle of cinematic exploitation; if necessary, the public must be protected as a child would be. Children should not be treated with contempt.

The glory of *Les Visiteurs du Soir* made us too easily forget the importance of *La Nuit Fantastique* in French film production since the war. The merit and the courage of making the first dent in the idiotic production of the time, the merit also of having rehabilitated the marvelous, which was to triumph in *Les Visiteurs du Soir,* should be credited to Marcel L'Herbier's film.

The last masterpiece of French cinema had been *Le Jour Se Lève. La Nuit Fantastique* gave the signal for a reversal of steam that will have its importance in the history of French cinema.

Marcel L'Herbier was right to launch this reversal under the banner of Méliès. Indeed, *La Nuit Fantastique* seems like a return to both the historical and the technical sources of cinema. The history of the origins of an art always enlightens us about its essence. This brief period of exceptional vitality, of privileged effectiveness, which accompanies the birth of great inventions, like those of certain chemical compounds, makes it possible for them to find their ideal combinations very quickly. It is only afterward, when the artist begins to reflect on his art, the merchant on his merchandise, the scientist on his discovery, that everything begins to degenerate and the spirit goes astray. Let us not therefore attribute the conjunction of Méliès and cinema to chance; it is the cinema that found him, it is the cinema that elected him, in those paradisical days when it had not yet become the Seventh Art and thus had the infallibility of children.

Cinema was drawn to this pure-hearted magician, choosing him above all others as its father. Méliès gave cinema its childhood—a much too brief childhood—but the merchants and the hucksters, the swindlers and the academicians, came along. They had little trouble taking the cinema away from him. Didn't they have money, intelligence, and culture on

Filmed in 1942, Marcel L'Herbier's *La Nuit Fantastique* starred Micheline Presle and Fernand Gravey. Under the "banner of Méliès," it restored, after an era of realism, "one of the biological paths . . . of cinema." (French Cultural Services)

their side? The simple soul couldn't for very long keep the child found one evening at the door of the Grand Café. It was becoming clear that the kid would easily be able to enrich his guardian with both money and literary glory. A few years, therefore, were enough to ruin Méliès and tear cinema from his grasp, but this little bit of time had also been enough to allow the auteur of *Baron de Münchhausen* to discover and make use of all the basic possibilities of this new means of expression, to endow cinema with the marvelous, the impossible, the dream.

The situation of Marcel L'Herbier's film in relation to

Méliès' work explains both the film's interest and its limitations. Its interest because *La Nuit Fantastique* restores to us, after an era of realism, that which is perhaps the path—or at least one of the biological paths—of cinema. The average film-goer is a person without memory. So far as he's concerned, all cinema is contained in the current season, in the year's distribution. L'Herbier's film also represents cinema's limitations, because, alas, certain experiences cannot be renewed, being inseparable from the spiritual conditions of their origin. Méliès is a primitive. He is the Douanier Rousseau of cinema. The work of Marcel L'Herbier [3] has none of the freshness of style, of spirit, that makes for the charm of our magician's short reels, but this is not only because of the esthetic temperament of the auteur but because of independent historical reasons.

This lack is unfortunately not sufficiently compensated for by the successes that might be expected in the domain of intellectual fantasy. At no time does one enter the proposed game. To capture us, it would have been necessary to make the poetry of dreams tangible; it would have been necessary, to a certain extent, for the players themselves to enter into the game in order to pull us into it.

They don't seem to have managed this. The work remains as external to them as it is to us. I confess my deep disappointment where scenarists Louis Chavance and Maurice Henry are concerned. Yet the former is not a cinema novice, and of the latter, because of his connection to Surrealism, a little more boldness and sincerity of imagination might justly have been expected. As it happens, the somewhat zany passages are precisely the most uninspired ones. Indeed, failure of imagination remains the film's principal weakness, and this is particularly evident, for example, in the lunatic asylum, a situation from which neither a logical (if I may put it that way) nor a rhythmic advantage is drawn.

It's extremely curious to note the complete lack of rhythm in this film, which should have been treated in the tempo of an American comedy. In *L'Honorable Catherine* [4] Marcel L'Herbier proved to us that he is one of our most brilliant continuity technicians, but that was a commercial film, important only because of the skill of its cinematic *écriture*. One wonders, therefore, if it is not the subject itself and, perhaps, how strongly he was drawn to it, that interfered with the conception of the continuity of *La Nuit Fantastique*. Be that as it may, it is as much in the lack of rhythm as in the boldness of a disconcerting story that the commercial handicap of the work must be sought.

One can, at least, only wholeheartedly praise the plastic qualities of this realization, in which the suggestiveness and the beauty of the image naturally play a basic role. It goes without saying that it was precisely the most beautiful images that were cut when the film was shown in neighborhood theaters.

Attention should also be drawn to the excellent use made of sound effects, which Marcel L'Herbier employs with happy discretion. The famous scene of the inversion of words, and several shots suggesting Fernand Gravey's drunkenness by means of optical and sound overprints are most effective.

La Nuit Fantastique is among those films that are partial failures but about which one feels guilty at expressing reservations. There is, actually, a hierarchy of failures and successes. *La Nuit Fantastique* is at least a quality work that has the merit of greatly dominating overall current production by the style of its inspiration as well as by the intelligence of its methods. Because of this, it fully justified in its own time the Grand Prix de la Critique Cinématographique, and, more recently, the distinction of the Prix du Film d'Art. It remains a work that marks a date in cinema since the war, a work that one should see because its very weaknesses are richer in instruction than many more facile successes.

(May 20, 1944)

Notes

1. September 1943 saw the inauguration of IDHEC, France's first cinema school, something Marcel L'Herbier had been requesting for many years and from which in the following years were to come: Alain Resnais, Henri Colpi, Jean Aurel, Jacques Rozier, Serge Bourguignon, Louis Malle, Pierre Tchernia, Jean-Christophe Averty, Jean Lhote, François Billetdoux, etc. . . . (F.T.)

2. *La Nuit Fantastique*. Direction: Marcel L'Herbier. Scenario: Louis Chavance and Maurice Henry. Dialogue: Henri Jeanson. Actors: Micheline Presle, Fernand Gravey, Parédès, Saturnin Fabre, Michel Vitold, Bernard Blier.

3. Since the advent of sound, Marcel L'Herbier had directed *L'Enfant de l'Amour* (1929), *La Femme d'une Nuit* (1930), *Le Mystère de la Chambre Jaune* (1930), *Le Parfum de la Dame en Noire* (1931), *L'Epervier* (1933), *Le Scandale* (1934), *L'Aventurier* (1934), *Le Bonheur* (1934), *La Route Impériale* (1935), *Veille d'Armes* (1935), *Les Hommes Nouveaux* (1936), *La Porte du Large* (1936), *Nuits de Feu* (1936), *La Citadelle du Silence* (1937), *Forfaiture* (1937), *La Tragédie Impériale* (1938), *Adrienne Lecouvreur* (1938), *Terre de Feu* (1938), *L'Entente Cordiale* (1939), *La Mode Rêvée* (1939), *La Comédie du Bonheur* (1940), *Histoire de Rire* (1941), *La Nuit Fantastique* (1942), *L'Honorable Catherine* (1942).

4. *L'Honorable Catherine*. Adaptation: Marcel L'Herbier from a play by Solange Terac. Dialogue: Henri Jeanson. Actors: Edwidge Feuillère, Raymond Rouleau, André Luguet, Claude Génia, Hubert de Mallet.

The Cinema and Popular Art

Though there may be a difference of opinion about which century saw the beginnings of the slow disassociation that was to lead to the separation of art from the people, there is no contesting the fact that the nineteenth century had the privilege of consummating a divorce that counts as among the gravest symptoms of a crisis in civilization. Intellectuals have been much preoccupied, especially in the last decade, with the problem of popular art. On various grounds, often from different points of view and inspired by more or less pure intentions, they have tried to rediscover some points at which art and the people could be reintegrated. We have thus witnessed attempts at poetic, pictorial, or dramatic grafts whose interest cannot be denied, though none of them offer great hopes or give promise of success on a civilization-wide scale.

The strange thing is that the intellectuals, the theoreticians of these attempts, seem to forget that the modern world definitively found *its* popular art fifty years ago. The fact that attempts are made to popularize the novel, that interest has been shown in remedying the verbal and spiritual solitude in which modern poetry is struggling, that, above all, efforts have been made to regenerate the theater at the hearth of more popular commonalities—all this undoubtedly has an enormous bearing on the destiny of these arts; but sociologically it remains a secondary problem. The very fact that this problem has been posed by intellectuals, that it requires so many conflicting efforts to be resolved, that the results are so fragile and unpermanent, proves if not its illegitimate nature at least its deliberate and self-conscious one. On the other hand, only one art (and let us note that it is a new art)—born unexpectedly while nobody was paying attention, delivered over to the competition of adventurers from all cultures, of all origins, who know no other law than that of material success—only one art has conquered the Western world in twenty years, the entire planet in thirty years, giving birth to the second worldwide industry. Only one art has grown, through its vitality alone, like a force of nature. Its esthetic value, the quality of its spiritual contribution, can undoubtedly be disputed, but there is no arguing the fact that the entire world has acquired a popular art thanks to the cinema.

But this observation poses, alas, a certain number of problems that it would be useful to become aware of. Within the limitations of this article, I would like to formulate only one, which is perhaps the basis of all the others.

Until the nineteenth century the notion of popular art was inseparable from that of community. The more limited and differentiated the human group to which it corresponds, the less assimilable it is to other human groups, the more popular is a dance, a song, a story, a style of furniture or of house. Popularity in this case is understood in the sense of the particular and the intensive. It finds expression in tradition and ritual.

In modern civilization, however, and especially where cinema is concerned, the concept of popularity takes on a completely different meaning. A film is the more popular the more directly it is assimilable by the greatest number of people on the surface of the earth, to its very ends, as has often happened; the Chinese coolie of the suburbs of Shanghai, the African black, the European, the Yankee, of all classes, of all intellectual formations, even of all ages—all get pleasure from it. Popularity is here understood in the extensive sense. It is measured by the space conquered, by the number of people it reaches.

The meaning and the consequences of this phenomenon do not seem to have been sufficiently studied. We will hazard only an esthetic observation about it.

The relationship of the artist to the consumer has been radically overturned. Popular folk art is born slowly from a social group: it *necessarily* expresses that group. Creation and use are so closely dependent on one another as to suggest an organic spontaneity that guarantees the perfect suitability of the work to the man. Cinema, however, because it does not spring from a communal psychology but from a sociology of atomized and gregarious masses, cannot benefit from such spontaneous generation. The suitability of the work to the consumer can only be the result of an obscure and infallible thrust of which the craftsman or the artist is only the interpreter. At most, it may be said that the popular need, for all intents and purposes, exists as an invisible need that the work may satisfy but by which it can never be automatically molded.

It is this absence of positive internal necessity that explains why we have as yet found in cinema only a means of expression and not a satisfying content. It also explains why the problem of popular art is not resolved by the mere appearance of a popular art. The popular works of the future will necessarily be cinematic. It would be dangerous to believe that they will necessarily find their material without the at least negative intervention of an esthetic politic. The fate of cinema is partially comparable to that of that other eminently social art: architecture. Abandoned to itself, the latter comes up with That'll-do Manor or a building whose function it is to show a profit; on its own, cinema comes up with Emile Couzinet or Fernandel films.

A humanistic cinema and urbanism have to be prepared for. Only the filmmaker and the architect can be counted on to do this. The consumer is definitely excluded from the process of creation. The importance of the technical advances that will soon be available cannot be denied, but will they really change the fundamentals of the problem, which it seems to me were posed in their entirety in the time of the Lumière brothers and Méliès? On the one hand these fundamentals are linked to the realism, the automatic objectivity, of the cinematic image; on the other hand they arise from the economic and social conditions that impose cinema's popular vocation on it.

The circumstances that determine cinema make it pointless to hope that a free play of production, influenced only by commercial success (the supposed expression of consumer satisfaction), will bring about some kind of progress in the esthetic value of film. On the other hand, it would be utopian to think that a reform, an education of the spectator on the level of the masses where the problem is posed, can ever be effective. The motive force of all progress remains on the side of creation. This doesn't mean that such education of the public is not to be undertaken, but like literary culture, it finds sufficient justification in itself. The millions of film-goers will always be without positive influence on the creative process. Of course, where technical quality is concerned, we need not worry. Cinema participates in the same determinism of progress as all modern machines. We will have color as surely as we had the vacuum cleaner, and 3-D is as inevitable as the airplane. Perfection in this domain is certain; one need only let events take their course. But when it comes to things of a spiritual nature, there is nothing to suggest a spontaneous advance of artistic quality where a mass art is concerned.

The future of cinema, like that of radio, is therefore dependent on a cultural politic. The modalities of this politic are obviously still to be discovered if this esthetic planning is not to work against its goals. Perhaps it should be limited to a sort of guardianship of quality. Perhaps it should be reinforced by having good films profit from financial measures such as tax abatements. Perhaps domestic films should be economically protected against foreign competition. In any case, the future of cinema will be much more dependent on the influences exercised at the creative level than on the reactions of the consumer.

This does not mean, however, that this art should be cut off from the people. The worthwhile works of tomorrow, like those of yesterday, will satisfy the fundamental aspirations of the modern public; they will be significant because of a deep harmony between the work and the people of our time. The creator will remain he in whom these silent appeals of the world will have resonated and who will nourish his work on them. Even in satire and revolt, cinema remains in the service of society; but it can only be so by truly expressing it, not by that intellectual demagogy which attempts to make us confuse the popularity of works with their spiritual poverty.

To express society, one must first of all represent it with care for material exactitude and moral authenticity. This is not an apologia for realism, because even a cinema of escape and fantasy benefits from remaining in the grain of reality. Doesn't the effectiveness of [Alain-Fournier's novel] *Le Grand Meaulnes* stem in part from the fact that the truth about the French landscape and people is more faithfully respected in that novel than in the work of Zola? The very nature of cinema pledges it to expressing the eternal only in the details of the moment; and "the exactitudes of backgrounds" as our colleague Claude Jacquier says in *Confluences,* plays an important role in this. Now, nine out of ten of our films present a horrifyingly false image of contemporary French society, an image that is all the more pernicious in that we are unaware of its falseness.

Moralists should realize that the chief danger of cinema may reside in this demagogic mythology in which society believes itself represented and to which it ends by unconsciously conforming. We eventually become so accustomed to this falsification that we have trouble imagining what a revolution this will to exactitude would bring about in the style of the decor and in the conception of the mise-en-scène.

Let us remember that in our world, when it comes to participating in various social milieus, people have practically no means but the cinema of knowing one another. A French farmer who had gone to the movies in the county seat every Sunday would know much more about the life of an American worker than about that of his Parisian equivalent. This same French worker—what does he know of the middle class, of the private life of a milieu to which he has no access, except that which he has basically learned in the cinema? Of course for a society to be expressed it must first exist—in other words, it must have a soul, a minimum of coherence, of unity, of a desire to be or become. The fate of a popular art is inseparable from social destiny, but it must contribute to the awareness of this destiny; instead it too often misleads us. This is a problem of social spirituality that transcends any necessity of specific political propaganda. Don't we also find it in every historical stage of the theater? It would be easy to demonstrate the ineluctable dialectic linking all great theatrical and cinematic works to the society they always express, even when the latter has not yet become aware of itself. (*L'Information Universitaire*—June 25, 1944)

The Balance Sheet for the 1943–44 Season

And so *Les Petites du Quai aux Fleurs* will have brought the cinematic season to a close. In a mediocre fashion, alas! This film will add nothing to the reputation of Marc Allégret, nor to that of Marcel Achard and Jean Aurenche.[1] How could the collaboration of these talented scenarists and dialoguists with the director of *Lac-aux-Dames* (1934) and *Entrée des Artistes* (1938) have resulted in this run-of-the-mill work that hasn't even the minimum of technical virtuosity which provided the interest, completely formal, that partially redeemed Christian-Jaque's *Voyage sans Espoir*?

The neutrality of this film, which is neither good nor very bad, rather exactly describes the tone of French film production during the last few months. The balance sheet we prepared earlier in the academic year noted the astonishing recovery of French cinema in 1942–43. The curve has evidently taken a significant downward turn.

September gave us *L'Eternel Retour*. This Delannoy film belonged to the previous year's production. Its release strengthened the link between the two seasons, suitably transmitting the flame—or rather the torch—lit by *Les Visiteurs du Soir*. Its luster made it possible for us to wait two or three months.

The same period saw the release of a film by Pierre and Jacques Prévert—*Adieu Léonard*—whose failure was complete (and to our way of thinking, justified). We would not mention it if it did not in fact confirm the sterility of what must be called—since it corresponds to a historical reality— a certain Café de Flore spirit. Though we don't want to draw from this unhappy experience overgeneralized conclusions about the Saint-Germain-des-Prés coteries, we can however take note of them.

L'Eternel Retour was about to leave the first-run houses when an impressive advertising campaign announced Pierre Billon's *Vautrin*.[2] This respectable film was no doubt not quite up to its subject; however, thanks to a certain technical probity it could be seen without boredom. *Le Voyage sans Espoir*, the only Christian-Jaque film we've had this year, confirmed the mastery of its auteur, especially in the exposition sequences—true anthology pieces. But this rhetorical skill emphasized the poverty of a script unworthy of this director.[3]

February gave us hope with *Le Ciel Est à Vous*, the only film of the season comparable to the four or five great successes of the previous seasons. This disconcerting work, with its apparently conventional and uplifting subject, proved that Jean Grémillon's technical virtuosity could completely efface itself in a realistic style that was deliberately neutral, invisible, capable of giving us the illusion of life without at any time making us feel that the lens was an intermediary. It is great praise indeed to say that this film reminds us of Jean Renoir's extraordinary *Le Crime de Monsieur Lange*.

Premier de Cordée, the new Daquin film, was awaited with impatience. Sympathetic *a priori* both because of the personality of its auteur and the spirit that had gone into its realization, this work was unfortunately to disappoint us. At no time is the presence of the mountain really felt. Now, films of this kind must be solidly based on natural, documentary, foundations. It is perhaps also true, and this is more serious, that Daquin, whose taste is so sure when it comes to the details of a sequence, lack vigor when it comes to overall film design. Daquin's great film is still to come, but he is the man to make it.

After several dismal weeks we also got *Le Carrefour des Enfants Perdus,* in which Léo Joannon managed to draw from a conventional subject a very popular work that had a sympathetic verve. And finally, after according two honorable mentions to two pleasant little films—*Bonsoir Mesdames, Bonjour Messieurs* [4] and *L'Aventure Est au Coin de la Rue* [5] —we have exhausted the honors list for the year. Let us just mention an honest film like Joannon's *Lucrèce* and a "quality" film, *Le Voyageur sans Bagage*—which we hope will have wearied Anouilh with cinema—and we will have come to the end.[6]

Though the previous season had revealed Clouzot, Bresson, and Becker, and had so brilliantly confirmed the talent of Grémillon and Autant-Lara that it seemed almost to reveal them anew, the year 1943–44 on the contrary lacks new men and original works. Is French cinema then content to just let itself be carried along on the stream?

We think that it would be unfair to judge it only on this balance sheet, without more seriously studying the items in its dossier.

Let us first of all take into account that considerably fewer films have been produced; less than thirty licenses were issued (scarcely half that of the two previous years), and of that number only little more than twenty were actually completed. If we consider the proportion of good films and not their absolute number, we must be less severe. Let us also not forget that commercial exploitation doesn't necessarily correspond to the reality of this production. For example, economic or political factors in these last few months prevented the release of Christian-Jaque's *Carmen* with Jean Marais and Viviane Romance (an Italian production, it is true), and of Marcel Carné's *Les Enfants du Paradis.*[7] These are important and no doubt decisive gaps in the artistic balance of the season. Finally, let us remember that in the last few months electricity restrictions have forced our studios to live at a slower pace and that thus six or seven films of the quota, which should have already been released, have not been completed and are still in the works. Let's cite from among them Marc Allégret's *Lunegarde,* P. de Herain's *Pamela,* Robert Vernay's *Le Père Goriot,* Robert Bresson's *Les Dames du Bois de Boulogne,* Christian-Jaque's *Sortilèges,* Jacques Becker's *Falbalas,* Pierre Billon's *Mademoiselle X,* etc. As can be seen from this list—on which do not figure projects which were launched some time ago but which like Claude Autant-Lara's *Sylvie et le Fantôme*[8] never got past the shooting script stage—the physiognomy of our movie theater programs does not at all correspond to the reality of our production, in which our best directors have been prevented from taking normal advantage of their opportunities.

Our cinema, therefore, should not be too quickly judged on the basis of a relatively mediocre season. It is even possible to believe that the health and probably the quality of our production has remained sound in spite of terrible economic and technical conditions. French cinema is putting up an almost miraculous fight, with a vitality and energy that may perhaps surprise its historians. French cinema is not dead, or even asleep; its silence is a knightly vigil of arms.

But production itself is not enough to give an idea of cinematic life in recent months. Though its films are limited in number, our cinema has demonstrated its will to live in other ways. I am thinking particularly of the birth of an institution that may have an extremely important influence on its future. The Institut des Hautes Etudes Cinématographiques (IDHEC) is making an attempt—for the first time in history, in the country of Lumière and Méliès—to methodically train filmmakers. The studio crafts have reached sufficient professional maturity to make it both possible and necessary to assure them a quota of personnel selected and trained according to the laws that are beginning to emerge from the history and techniques of the Seventh Art. Not only will cinema get new men, recruited in social and intellectual milieus to which it previously made little appeal, but in the course of providing instruction it will also become aware of itself. An art only achieves perfection in relation to this awareness, without which it cannot be transmitted; the teaching of the humanities is at the foundation of all our literature. As for the danger of academicism that some like to invoke, it is nothing more than a danger; it is not endemic to an instruction that can be carried on in a living and realistic contact with the true artists of our cinema.

To the Institut des Hautes Etudes Cinématographiques and to the Service des Etudiants, we are also indebted for several initiatives limited by circumstances but important in principle. The film showings at which the director presents his film to students; the various lectures on the technique, esthetic, and history of cinema; and the creation of study groups within student centers have all launched an overall movement, a current of interest favoring this "school for the spectator" that the prewar clubs had for all practical purposes reserved for an elite of very knowledgeable film lovers.

It is comforting—at a time when our screens are darkening and in which despite an ingenious and tenacious struggle against events French cinema cannot escape paralysis—to note that basically it has not failed to live up to last year's promises and that though there are few films, we are at least left with substantial hopes. (July 8, 1944)

Notes

1. *Les Petites du Quai aux Fleurs* is a comedy featuring Odette Joyeux, Louis Jourdan, Bernard Blier, Daniel Delorme, and Gerard Philippe.

2. From Balzac's *Splendeurs et Misères des Courtisanes,* and featuring Michel Simon in the role of Vautrin.

3. *Voyage sans Espoir.* Direction: Christian-Jaque. Scenario: Pierre MacOrlan. Actors: Jean Marais, Simone Renant, Paul Bernard, Louis Salou, Lucien Cordel, Jean Brochard. Since the beginning of the Occupation, Christian-Jaque had directed: *L'Assassinat du Père Noël, Premier Bal, La Symphonie Fantastique, Carmen.*

4. Directed by Roland Tual from a scenario by Robert Desnos, who had already been deported when the film was released. The author of three thousand radio advertising slogans, Desnos could say: "I am the poet most listened to in Europe." Turning to the cinema, he did *Bonsoir Mesdames, Bonjour Messieurs,* a comedy about radio broadcasting. Desnos died in the Nazi concentration camp of Terezin in Czechoslovakia. (F.T.)

5. Directed by Jacques Daniel Norman.

6. *Le Voyageur sans Bagage,* written and directed by Jean Anouilh and based on his own play. Actors: Pierre Fresnay, Blanchette Brunoy, Pierre Renoir, and Jean Brochard.

7. *Les Enfants du Paradis* was not to be completed until after the Liberation. Robert Le Vigan, originally cast in the role of Jericho, the Old Clothes Man-Fate, left France for Argentina (after having accompanied L.F. Céline to Sigmarigen and having been acquitted by the Purification Tribunals), and was replaced by Pierre Renoir. (F.T.)

8. *Sylvie et le Fantôme,* adaptation and dialogue by Jean Aurenche from a play by Alfred Adam, was directed by Claude Autant-Lara after the war in 1945. Actors: Odette Joyeux, François Perier, and Jacques Tati (in the role of the phantom).

3 : THE LIBERATION
   AND THE TRANSITION

Reflections for a Vigil of Arms

Since electricity restrictions force us, for all intents and purposes, to mark time on the threshold of the Promised Land of American cinema, since our studios have been obliged to suspend operations and the Liberation Committee is still as I write suffering the difficult birth pangs of new institutions, there is time for meditation and an examination of conscience.

For two years now critics have unanimously and unceasingly been congratulating themselves on the progress of French cinema. Just think back to 1940–41 film production, the nothingness of which skirted disaster. We were ready to believe that our cinema was condemned. But even as we listened to the demon of despair, there was already being erected under the sky of Provençe the great white chateau that Marcel Carné was to make the bastion of our hopes. They were not to be disappointed: three years of wartime production today reveal themselves as not only honorable but of an exceptional richness.

And yet that war had amputated from us our greatest directors—Renoir, Duvivier, Feyder, and our most tested stars —Gabin and Michèle Morgan. In spite of Carné, who did not in fact show himself unworthy of his past, we were not to encounter works comparable to *La Grande Illusion, La Bête Humaine, Pépé le Moko,* or *La Kermesse Héroïque.* But their absence has not been without a positive aspect. Faced with the necessity of replacing the exiles, French cinema permitted a pleiade of young technicians to show their worth, men who might otherwise perhaps have remained in the shadow of the great masters. (A producer, of course, does not like to take a chance on new names, and we are no longer, or are not yet, in a stage of experimental cinema.) Thus there came to the fore the Daquin of *Nous les Gosses,* the Becker of *Dernier Atout* and *Goupi Mains Rouges,* the

Clouzot of *Le Corbeau*, and the Bresson of *Les Anges du Péché*. Some veterans, who until then had remained in the second rank, also had a chance to show that they were better than we thought. Claude Autant-Lara with his 1900 trilogy—*Mariage de Chiffon, Lettres d'Amour*, and *Douce*; Grémillon with *Lumière d'Eté* and especially with *Le Ciel Est à Vous*; Delannoy (assisted by Cocteau) with *L'Eternel Retour*, some aspects of which equal *Les Visiteurs du Soir*; and Christian-Jaque, whose extraordinary technical skill has unfortunately continued to deteriorate from *L'Assassinat du Père Noël* to *Carmen*.

This production is not only not inferior to that of the prewar period, but even marks a net proportional advance, considering that production was amputated by from 50 to 75 percent. Perhaps we weren't given the very great works that only a Renoir or a Feyder were capable of, but this lack was compensated for by the number of films of stature that have undeniably raised the level of our production.

It would be unjust to overlook the minor genres and particularly the documentary, which in three years has given us a considerable number of excellent exemplars. It seemed as if this form—of secondary importance economically, but fundamental to cinematic esthetics—was finally going to develop both style and status. We've hardly had much time to get to know Grimaud's cartoon characters—but there's been time enough to see that in the native land of Emile Cohl and Emile Reynaud there was a possibility that film animation might be reborn.

At a time when this production of which we are so proud is about to face world competition, we must admit to some uneasiness. Faced by a reality that has until now been too far off to have had much influence on our judgments, our optimism must henceforth be more cautious. Criticism, in fits of masochism, was from time to time undoubtedly aware that we had been unable to keep up with the technical advances abroad; that our industrial equipment would necessarily have become antiquated; that the various improvements in film, the practical evolution of cinema in terms of color and perhaps 3-D, television—that all this was going to surprise us before we were physically and intellectually prepared. This pessimism, which was perhaps not always unrelated to a more basic defeatism, is proving itself more or less baseless. American color production, which was thought to account for 75 percent of the total production, represents no more than 30 to 40 percent. Most of the great Hollywood works are still in black and white. As of now, the three-soundtrack film exists only as a prototype, and its use is not about to become widespread. It is not then the technical revolutions comparable to sound that threaten the immediate future of French film production.

There is, of course, the play of the economy. "Moreover," as Malraux says, "the cinema is an industry." The second world industry. Of all the arts, only cinema is dependent on this monstrous body which compromises its spiritual salvation. It is still too early to measure the dangers our cinema can expect from the more or less free play of world economic competition. But it would be hypocritically easy at this early stage to grow teary-eyed about its fate, as though the latter depended exclusively on the correlation of forces, of material conjunctures independent of its artistic value. Let's not pretend to close our eyes; our first weapon will be quality: a quality not understood in the narrow sense of formal perfection without depth, but a quality of inspiration without which style cannot attain to greatness. The fate of French cinema rests first and foremost in the hands of its artists; it will be determined by their genius.

A somewhat deeper examination of the esthetic tendencies of recent French production may perhaps give us the key to the uneasiness that is mixed with our praise of these four years of film production.

A captive nation that refused to exalt its slavery and yet

could not proclaim its desire for freedom naturally had to develop an escapist cinema. Thus we saw Carné, the "realist" of *Quai des Brumes,* of *Le Jour Se Lève,* and of *L'Hôtel du Nord,* renew himself in medieval fantasy. The greatest film of those four years is also the one that is furthest removed from them. Delannoy and Cocteau turn to legend; in spite of the modern transposition, *L'Eternel Retour* is so imprecise in time and space that it has no connection to the present day. *Douce, Le Mariage de Chiffon, La Duchesse de Langeais,* and *Les Anges du Péché* all borrow from history or from spiritual exile the prestige of a social or moral uprooting. The list of less important films, from *La Nuit Fantastique* to *Le Baron Fantôme,* including all the adaptations of Balzac and Maupassant, would confirm the same tendencies. We have had only three realist films: *Goupi Mains Rouges, Le Corbeau,* and *Le Ciel Est à Vous*; and even this minority kind of production was as independent of present-day events as the major part.

The public wanted the screen to be its window and not its mirror. The result was this paradoxical phenomenon: the social art par excellence—the one that drew together the greatest number of people, the most realistic art in terms of its means of expression—is the one to least express contemporary French society. In spite of the constraints of censorship, it would certainly have been possible to produce films which had no precise political tendency but in which some of the public's problems would have been portrayed. But the public would not have tolerated it. The universe of French cinema was suspended in 1939, just as the ball in *Les Visiteurs du Soir* was suspended. Once or twice a week the average filmgoer abandoned his flirtation with life for a couple of hours to once more take his place in the quadrille of his dreams. While all the militant functions of art took refuge in a more or less clandestine literature (in which, moreover, the general public had no part), the cinema drew to itself an oppressed people's appetite for escape.

And men are still oppressed, if only by life itself. Dreams will remain their basic expectation from the screen. But the escape that the French cinema will dispense for us tomorrow can no longer be the same. "What freedom may perhaps restore," Claude Roy wrote recently, "is a realistic cinema in the very tradition of French cinema and perhaps in the very tradition of French art in general." There is no reason why our directors cannot draw from the pain and hopes of these four years the inspiration for several great films; we even believe that the immediate future of our cinema depends on this. No reason, provided that they also prove themselves capable of suggesting new dreams to us. We are no longer interested in the same dreams.

It is a mistake to oppose realism to escapism; Alain-Fournier's novel *Le Grand Meaulnes* draws its strength from an exact evocation of the French countryside. It is this factor that often distinguishes worthwhile escapism from shoddy pipedreams. It is in any case what must characterize the escapism that we expect of the French cinema of tomorrow, because what we had asked for yesterday was perhaps not so much escape as an exile. Escapist cinema does not exclude the use of the contemporary scene. And we mean by that not events but primarily the spiritual actuality that they determine. Pétain's speech in *La Fille du Puisatier* [1] does not make that movie a film about contemporary events. What must be sought, either with or without the help of a realism established by details of the plot, are the deepest levels of the collective soul, in order that they be made conscious. This is not a plea for propaganda (the latter intervenes to direct liberated energy to a precise goal), but only for authenticity.

Despite its very important qualities, for the last four years our cinema has been marked by a social exile that has diluted its sap. If the incontestable artistic value, the suppleness and exactitude of our cinema's style, are to survive under their new circumstances, they must adapt to the new climate. We cannot stand up against the gust of grandeur, violence, hate, tenderness, and hope that will sweep over us with the American cinema unless we too set down the deepest roots in the soul of our time—in its angers and its sorrows as well as in its dreams. French cinema will only save itself if it learns how to become even greater by rediscovering an authentic expression of French society (*Poésie 44*—July-October 1944)

Notes
1. In Marcel Pagnol's *La Fille du Puisatier,* the first film begun after the Germans entered France, we see the characters gathered around a radio and listening to the Armistice speech made by Marshal Pétain. (F.T.)

Paris Screens

As we know, the Direction Générale du Cinéma and the Comité d'Organisation de l'Industrie Cinématographique having been dissolved and immediately taken over by the F.F.I. [French Forces of the Interior], the Comité de Libération du Cinéma Français, presided over by Pierre Blanchar and directed by Jean Painlevé, is in charge of the interim period between the previous institutions and the future ones. The task is a hard one, for it is not limited to the purification of the organization. What must be done is to reorganize French cinema on new foundations, and as can be imagined, the human, political, economic, and technical problems thus raised are extremely complex.

Several directors whose collaboration with Continentale has been particularly shocking or inopportune have already been placed under a ban. Among them are Henri Decoin (auteur of *Les Inconnus dans la Maison*) and Clouzot, whose *Le Corbeau* was distributed in Germany under the title *A French Town*.[1]

Outside the Comité de Libération, an unofficial corporative agitation has been developing in the profession.

Film producers, perhaps fearful of seeing their economic role in the cinema of tomorrow diminished, have held a noisy meeting from which nothing very clear seems to have resulted.

The directors held another meeting, at which was expressed the desire that M. Richebé no longer be authorized to dishonor French film production.

The distributors are anxiously trying to prove their usefulness.

While waiting for the American films, you can already go to the cinema if you have the courage to confront the impressive lines. The Comité de Libération is showing at the Normandie and the Gaumont a few collections of Allied newsreels and a report on the Resistance in Paris. The latter film cannot help but be deeply moving.

If, however, we may be permitted to criticize on a technical level a film whose human interest remains immense, let us express some regret that the editing is confused and the shots rarely very significant. It seems that an unfortunate economy of film has been practiced in a genre which by definition demands the greatest prodigality. Nevertheless, let us render homage to the courage of the cameraman and particularly point out a sequence of a cruel beauty: the one in which a German soldier crawls along a deserted street while all around him bullets spatter against the pavement like raindrops in a storm.

The new version, which for several days now has been playing at the Normandie, is perceptibly better than the first version in terms of both editing and the choice of shots.

(*Le Parisien Libéré*—September 10, 1944)

Notes

1. What the Comité d'Epuration [Purification Committee] particularly held against Henri Decoin (director of *Les Inconnus dans la Maison,* adapted by Clouzot from a Simenon novel) and Clouzot himself, was having turned to the Germany company Continentale in order to produce some of their films.

Continentale produced 30 of the 220 films made during the Occupation—the most significant being *Le Corbeau.* The underground press accused *Le Corbeau* of being anti-French and of having served Nazi propaganda purposes; it was rumored that *Le Corbeau* had been distributed in Germany under the title: *A Little Town in France.* After the war, appearing before the Comité d'Epuration, Louis Chavance, co-scenarist of the film, proved that a) his scenario had been written and registered in 1937, and b) that the film had never been shown in Germany, the German distributors of UFA having judged it too harsh. But the dispute continued, principally between Georges Sadoul—who thought that the auteurs of *Le Corbeau* should have made the film *before* the war or *after,* but not during—and directors Marcel Carné, Claude Autant-Lara, and Marcel L'Herbier, all of whom defended Clouzot and protested against the ban on the film (which remained in effect until 1946). It is because they too had been judged anti-French that *Quai des Brumes* and *La Règle du Jeu* had been banned during the year that preceded the war just as *Le Crime de Monsieur Lange, Le Jour Se Lève* and *Le Corbeau* were after the Liberation. (F.T.)

The Future of French Cinema

Yesterday, in order to explain its work and its projects, the Comité de Libération du Cinéma summoned all film professionals to the Gaumont theater.

Pierre Blanchar, president of the Comité de Libération du Cinéma, about to depart for England and the United States, where he is to present the film on the Resistance in Paris, opened the meeting, during which Jean Painlevé, now charged with the direction of French Cinema, and Louis Daquin, chairman of the Comité de Libération, spoke.

Louis Daquin expressed the intentions of the Comité as follows: to defend French cinema as a national spiritual patrimony; to assure its technical and moral quality with the aid of noncommercial agencies of technical control and by the institution of a sort of syndical council empowered to decide on the competence and the professional honor of members of the corporation; to reform the statute dealing with the film auteur, which had suffered under the decrees of Richebé; to maintain and develop the principle of the national Cinémathèque and of a national School of Cinema; to encourage the distribution of film shorts in rural areas as one of the most likely means to draw together farmers and city dwellers; and, finally and above all, to immediately create a production cooperative within whose framework some fifteen films have already been envisioned.

(*Le Parisien Libéré*—September 17, 1944)

Revival of Marcel Carné's Quai des Brumes

As we know, several weeks ago Captain Lhéritier, the military censor, banned Jean Renoir's *Le Crime de Monsieur Lange* and Marcel Carné's *Le Jour Se Lève*. The surety of judgment with which Captain Lhéritier has chosen from the many films submitted to him two of the best productions of French cinema in the last ten years utterly invalidates the charges of artistic incompetence that some people would like to level against the office of the censor, that venerable institution which Vichy itself had not dared to destroy. In any case, the vigilance of the censor must have been circumvented, and you can see a revival of Marcel Carné's *Quai des Brumes* [1] on the screen of Les Portiques.

It's an instructive venture: first, because it's better to *resee* a film than to see a bad film for the first time; second, because the perspective of several years makes it possible to judge what is lasting in a film and what evaporates with the taste and sensibility of a given epoch. In spite of its qualities, *Quai des Brumes* has not completely resisted the passage of time. The atmospheric realism, to which Carné and Prévert had given an effective and precise style, now reveals its lack of basic authenticity. It is removed from us, like a prewar convention, which in addition to everything else is inseparable from Gabin's strong personality: that of the tough guy, violent and tender, pursued through the fog of ports, the glacial water of rainy streets, the seedy hotel rooms, by an inner necessity that inexorably destines him to murder (past, as in *Quai des Brumes,* present, as in *Le Jour Se Lève,* or future, as in *La Bête Humaine*).

Nevertheless there would be a valid poetry in this character, an authentic tragedy in this fate, if the inspiration behind it were more sincere, if the source of it weren't in Saint-Germain-des-Prés, in that Café de Flore which has done so much good and so much harm to French cinema.

Go see *Quai des Brumes* again; it is one of our most beautiful films, and made with a master's hand. In it you will rediscover "our" Gabin (not the puffy and graying one of *Péniche de l'Amour*), the fathomless eyes of Michèle Morgan . . . May you not find it too different from what you remember.   (*Le Parisien Libéré*—November 19, 1944)

Notes

1. Direction: Marcel Carné. Scenario: Jacques Prévert, from the novel by Pierre MacOrlan. Dialogue: Jacques Prévert. Camerawork: Schuftan, assisted by Louis Page, Marc Fossard, Henri Alekan, Philippe Agostini.

Sets: Trauner. Music: Maurice Jaubert. Actors: Jean Gabin, Michèle Morgan, Michel Simon, Pierre Brasseur, Robert Le Vigan, Aimos, Delmont, Pérès, René Génin. Production: Grégor Rabinovitch (1938).

Waiting for Hollywood . . .

The Groupe des Etudes Américaines and the Groupe du Cinéma sponsored at the Maison des Lettres on February 3rd a lecture by Jean Mitry on American cinema of the past four years. The lecturer, a professor at the Institut des Hautes Etudes Cinématographiques, is one of the few historians of cinema, and he has all the documentation it is presently possible to have about American film production.

How many films have the Americans made since 1940? 3,000? 4,000? (In France, the specialists in the most favored positions have not seen more than ten of them, and those not of the greatest.)

Of this entire enormous production, undoubtedly all that will be remembered are some hundred interesting films and five or six masterpieces of the stature of *Jezebel* or *Stagecoach*. Add to this number about twenty films that are very good. Let's hope we will shortly see the most remarkable of them: *The Great Dictator, Air Force, The Long Voyage Home . . .*

What have the great directors been doing? John Ford at least (the auteur of *The Informer* and *Stagecoach*) is offering an authentic masterpiece, which actually goes back to 1940— *The Grapes of Wrath,* taken from a novel by Steinbeck.

That same year also gave us *The Long Voyage Home,* which we will see very soon: an admirable atmospheric film, "made of nothing," made solely of the fear of men on a munitions cargo going from New York to Liverpool.

Ford did away with everything that was "external." When the German planes attack near the English coast we do not see them; we see only the traces of the machinegun bullets, we hear only the noise. And an astonishing impression results from this concentration, from this deliberate schematization. A remarkable film also because of the images, the lighting, and the interpretation of light.

Let's cite a few other Ford titles as well: *Tobacco Road, How Green Was My Valley*. From Fritz Lang we have *Hangmen Also Die, Ministry of Fear*. From King Vidor, the vast historical fresco, *An American Romance*.

Frank Capra, after a series of documentaries, has done a satirical comedy. His last film, *Arsenic and Old Lace,* is the ironic and biting presentation of a story that could be handled as a somber drama.

And suppose we talk of *Gone With the Wind*? This four-hour film is a magnificent and captivating work . . . but it is not, properly speaking, a masterpiece. The best parts are not superior to the equivalent sections of *In Old Chicago*. The psychology, the dialogue, but not the images, whose role is purely descriptive.

The color, a little brutal and harsh at the beginning of the film—the making of which took over a year—becomes more and more authentic and real. The interior scenes, which evince a deliberate stylization, are, with their sepias, their blackish-browns, their warm tints, excellent examples of what might be called "black and white in colors." And since that film, color has continued to make progress in this direction.

An interesting tendency to point out: contemporary writers are playing a greater and greater role in the cinema. We have mentioned Steinbeck and Faulkner. Directors are asking authors to create scenarios. And authors are taking an interest in the cinema, in the overall style of the film. Sometimes they intervene directly in the mise-en-scène.

In conclusion, let us, following Jean Mitry's lead, note "the two currents" of American cinema. In addition to the great

works, frankly realistic and violent, often inspired by Steinbeck and Faulkner, another inspiration, born under the influence of the war, is noticeable: it is the basis of a pseudo-
spiritualist current, of films in which there is a concern for
problems of death and afterlife. (*Here Comes Mr. Jordan*
is an example.) A far from insignificant inspiration—though
often somewhat facile—since in any given year there may be
a good thirty films belonging to this type.

(*Courrier de l'Etudiant*—February 1, 1945)

Marcel Carné's Les Enfants du Paradis

Marcel Carné's film is undoubtedly the most important
cinematographic event that French film production has
known in the last two years. In the absence of Renoir, Feyder
and René Clair, Marcel Carné is incontestably our best director. He has been able, especially since the war, to renew himself with such boldness that *Les Visiteurs du Soir,* and now
Les Enfants du Paradis,[1] have advanced the frontiers of
French cinema.

To tell the truth, unlike *Les Visiteurs du Soir, Les Enfants
du Paradis* owes its originality much less to inspiration than
to form. Actually, with this subject, which is of a somewhat
melodramatic realism, Carné and Prévert return to the social
vein of their former successes, but the unusual dimensions of
the work permit a stylistic finesse, a precision of psychological analysis, that the demands for simplification in a film of
normal length do not generally allow.

Even so, the three and a quarter hours it takes to project
Les Enfants du Paradis give a paradoxical impression of
meagreness and inadequacy. The auteurs appear to have had

Starring Jean-Louis Barrault as the mime Baptiste Debureau, *Les Enfants du Paradis* recreated the Paris of the Romantic era. Though he acknowledged the film's importance, Bazin obviously did not care for it. (French Cultural Services)

Arletty scored a triumph as the enigmatic Garance. In spite of its over-three-hour length, *Les Enfants du Paradis,* which reunited the talents of Carné and Prévert, gave "a paradoxical impression of meagreness and inadequacy." (French Cultural Services)

much more to say about their characters but to have given up
. . . having run out of film or time. This fresco, in which four
or five destinies are mingled, seems unfinished. Admittedly,
the touch is sure, of a rare intelligence, of a skillfully elliptical elegance—but it remains cold, and as though scornful of
our assent, of our love. The principal defect of this work is
that it is merely admirable.

Let's hope that the demands of commercial exploitation
don't make it necessary to show the two parts separately. The
first part, especially, suffers from a certain slowness, and
absolutely cannot do without its justification by the second.

(*Le Parisien Libéré*—March 30, 1945)

Notes

1. *Les Enfants du Paradis* (1943–1945). Direction: Marcel Carné.
Scenario: Jacques Prévert. Photography: Roger Hubert. Sets: Barsacq,
Gabutti, Trauner. Music: Joseph Kosma. Actors: Arletty, Jean-Louis
Barrault, Maria Casarès, Pierre Brasseur, Louis Salou, Marcel Herrand,
Pierre Renoir, Jane Marken.

In a letter to the translator, François Truffaut pointed out that
though Bazin obviously did not like the film, the small amount of space
devoted to it was entirely due to the paper restrictions at the time. He
noted that Bazin often did not care for a film on first seeing it—Robert
Bresson's *Les Dames du Bois de Boulogne* (1945), Jean Cocteau's *La
Belle et la Bête* (1946), and Jean Renoir's *The Diary of a Chambermaid*
(1946) are cases in point—but would become enthusiastic on reseeing it,
admitting as much in later articles. Aware of this, Truffaut reread
Bazin's later articles on Marcel Carné but found that they contain no
such change of opinion. Truffaut himself considers the film the best of
the Carné-Prévert collaborations. (S.H.)

Jaubert and French Cinema

On June 19th it will be five years since, in the early days of the war, struck down like [the poet Charles] Péguy at the head of his men by a machine-gun bullet, Captain Jaubert opened the book of the dead in which were to be inscribed the names of Jacques Decour, Politzer, Saint-Pol Roux, Max Jacob, Saint-Exupéry . . . "The purest of us is gone," wrote Claude-André Puget. "He takes with him a portion of the light of this world; those who have not known him cannot understand."

I am of those who did not know him—of those, however, who dare feel for him that almost familial affection that one has for the others who are gone, those whose human presence remains almost undiminished among us: Rivière, Alain-Fournier . . . He is of that same race of artists, so rare, whose work, even in its most objective forms, always remains the expression of a deep spiritual life. The result is that their souls remain accessible to us in spite of the absurdity of their corporeal absence.

The work of Maurice Jaubert is indeed inseparable from his most intimate personal qualities; his musical esthetic, in its principles and in its consequences, proceeds from a generosity, a sincerity, and, one might say, a basic charity of inspiration that refused to reject the joy of being alive; because of this, to the subtle rhetoric, to the pseudo-esthetic esotericism that threatened to overwhelm music, he opposed the determination to make it possible for his contemporaries to one day encounter the music of their time. "We demand," he said, "a popular music, and contrary to appearances that does not mean we are looking for the easy way. The real difficulty—and real courage as well—does not consist in hiding behind the mysteries of theory, but in rediscovering music in its most naked form so as to work at restoring to it the sense of human, and if possible, collective song."

He very quickly found in cinema the ideal ally of his musical esthetic. The new art, if one wanted to serve it honestly, to go with the grain of its basic nature without trickery and without pretense, was the popular art par excellence, the art of the largest audiences. Thus Jaubert, perhaps alone of all French musicians, came simultaneously to both cinema and music. Other musicians always more or less seem to make temporary incursions into the Seventh Art, or merely to lend their collaboration. Only of Jaubert can it be said that he belongs equally to cinema and to music.

Accepting from the beginning the rules of a game that completely saved the dignity of two arts, he seems to have applied and understood them with an unprecedented ease. He was without doubt the most productive of our screen musicians, since he began with an orchestra score for a silent film, *Le Mensonge de Nina Petrowna,* and the number of sound films for which he wrote music (*Quatorze Juillet, Le Dernier Milliardaire, Drôle de Drame, La Vie d'un Fleuve, Un Carnet de Bal, Quai des Brumes, Le Jour Se Lève*), is well over a hundred. "Many others," wrote Georges Auric, "in his place would have been satisfied—let's admit it, were satisfied—to improvise with a perhaps excusable skepticism what one wanted to see them write . . . But conserving a moving faith in an art, all thè possibilities of which he deeply felt, he managed to triumph over the worst obstacles." His cinematic competence, profound enough so that the greatest directors did not hesitate to turn to him for advice, and the certainty of his judgment, enabled him to resolve with a mastery that belonged to him alone the many problems raised by synchronization. Other musicians, and among them the greatest, have written for the cinema, but their greatest successes, compared to his, even when they equaled his, have an almost miraculous precariousness. Only Jaubert never seemed in danger of breaking the unity of the cinematic work. Think of the haunting music of *Quatorze Juillet,* the prodigious musical background of *Quai des Brumes.*[1]

This continuing and apparently so natural success was due to a profound understanding of the relationship between sound and image. The faultlessly skillful practitioner was also an exhaustive theoretician of his art. His several articles, and particularly a talk he gave in London (no French translation of which is yet available), define the role of film music with decisive clarity and intelligence. The union of musical and plastic rhythm, the harmony of the lyric commentary and the dramatic development—to all those problems which in other estheticians seem like squaring the circle he suggested solutions of an astonishing elegance. Denouncing musical redundancy, sentimental commentary, or imitative synchronism, fleeing facileness and eloquence, he insists that film music deepen the visual impression.

"We don't ask of music that it 'explain' the images but that it add to them a resonance of a specifically dissimilar nature. We don't ask music to be 'expressive' and to add its sentiment to that of the characters or the director, but to be 'decorative' and to join its own arabesque to that proposed to us by the screen. Let music finally rid itself of all its subjective elements, let it render physically sensible the internal rhythm of the image without trying to translate the sentimental, dramatic, or poetic content."

With Maurice Jaubert, French cinema has lost one of its great masters in terms of both talent and spirit. On the threshold of a new national production that awakens a great deal of uneasiness in us, it is well to think of Jaubert. Because he continually found the source of his inspiration and the rules of his technique in the highest respect for the cinematic work, in an equal love of both music and men, he is among those who worked hardest for the grandeur and the dignity of French cinema. His work is not only a credit to our purest artistic patrimony, but should today be a lesson of determination and purity for our cinema, and should help us retain our hopes.   (*Courrier de l'Etudiant*—May 1945)

Notes

1. Bazin is forgetting Jaubert's two splendid musical scores for Jean Vigo's *Zéro de Conduite* and *L'Atalante,* but I imagine that it was not until several months later that he discovered these films. (F.T.)

Julien Duvivier's Untel Père et Fils

Duvivier's film was completed in 1940 and could not be shown here during the Occupation for obvious reasons.[1]

It is the domestic saga of a French family from 1870 to 1940. To tell the truth the film is more like an album of animated photographs, like a collection of inevitable bravura pieces: the siege of Paris, the introduction of the bicycle, the automobile, the heroic days of aviation, the 1914 mobilization, the sickening euphoria of the postwar period, the colonial saga of the family adventurer who, after a disappointing love affair, ruins his health in building bridges in Equatorial Africa, the French can-can and the loan to Russia, and, to round things off, the mobilization of 1939 and the patriotic speech that recalls the one at the beginning when Jouvert, a National Guardsman, leaves for the offensive against the Prussian lines.

This historical fresco, imbued with a discreet and disillusioned patriotism, seems like something from another age. These last four years have completely overturned our judgments and our national sensibility. There is something painful in this exhumation of the sentiments of the "phony war."

A domestic saga of a French family from 1870 to 1940, Julien Duvivier's *Untel Père et Fils* (1940) could not be shown in France until after the Liberation and was released first in the United States as *The Heart of a Nation*. (French Cultural Services)

From an artistic point of view it is not the best Duvivier.[2] Except for two or three successful sequences like the one done in indirect style, dealing with the testing of planes, the images are generally of a facile and superficial eloquence.

The sumptuousness of the cast (Raimu, Morgan, Jouvet, Ledoux, Lucien Nat, etc. . . . .) will assure this film a success that it is bound to achieve whether it is good or bad.

(Le Parisien Libéré—October 23, 1945)

115 : *Julien Duvivier's* Untel Père et Fils

Notes

1. Scenario Adaptation: Marcel Achard, Charles Spaak, Julien Duvivier. Dialogue: Marcel Achard, Charles Spaak. Photography: J.
Kruger. Sets: Guy de Gastyne. Music: Jean Wiener. Costumes: Rosine
Delamare. Editing: Marthe Poncin. Actors: Raimu, Louis Jouvet, Michèle Morgan, Suzy Prim, Renée Devilliers, Robert Le Vigan, Jean
Mercanton, Lucien Nat, Harry Krimer, Colette Darfeuil, Pierre Magnier,
Louis Jourdan, Biscot, Fernand Ledoux, Daniel Mendaille, Anita Com-
bault, René Génin, Jean Mercury, Yvonne Legay, Raymone, and the
voice of Charles Boyer. Producer: Transcontinental (Paul Graetz) 1939,
1 hour, 55 minutes—Hollywood 1940 (under the title *Heart of a Nation*),
Paris, October 17, 1945.

2. From 1930 to 1940, Julien Duvivier directed *David Golder* (1931),
Les Cinq Gentlemen Maudits (1932), *Allo Berlin? Ici Paris!* (1932), *Poil
de Carotte* (1932), *La Tête d'un Homme* (1933), *Le Petit Roi* (1933),
Le Paquebot Tenacity (1934), *Maria Chapdelaine* (1934), *Golgotha*
(1935), *La Bandera* (1935), *L'Homme du Jour* (1936), *Le Golem* (1936),
La Belle Equipe (1936), *Pépé le Moko* (1937), *Un Carnet de Bal* (1937),
Toute la Ville Danse (1939), *La Charette Fantôme* (1939), *La Fin du
Jour* (1939), *Untel Père et Fils* (1940). In Hollywood he continued his
prolific career: *Lydia* (1941), *Tales of Manhattan* (1942), *Flesh and
Fantasy* (1943), *The Impostor* (1943), with Jean Gabin. (F.T.)

4 : FILMS OF
   THE RESISTANCE

Christian-Jaque's Boule de Suif

The first film [1] on the Resistance! A dangerous subject. Christian-Jaque [2] approached it by way of Guy de Maupassant and the historical transposition of the war of 1870.

It is perhaps this prudent perspective that makes the film more or less acceptable and allows us to half believe the misadventures of stagecoach voyagers grappling with Prussians and the "maquis" of 1871. No stereotype is completely avoided, but the intelligence of dialoguist Henri Jeanson at least spares us melodrama. The brilliant cast (especially Micheline Presle in the role of the sympathetic and courageous prostitute confronted by the pharisaism of middle-class collaborators) and the contemporaneity of the subject will assure this film a success that it partially merits.

Let's hope that Christian-Jaque has finally exorcised the stagecoach complex that has haunted him since *Stagecoach*. This time he has honestly preferred pastiche to plagiarism. The stagecoach in *Boule de Suif*, accompanied by the same musical theme that ran through John Ford's film, is, one might say, used between quotes. [3]

(*Le Parisien Libéré*—October 22, 1945)

Notes

1. *Boule de Suif,* drawn from Guy de Maupassant's "Boule de Suif" and "Mademoiselle Fifi." Direction: Christian-Jaque. Adaptation: Henri Jeanson and Louis d'Hée. Dialogue: Henri Jeanson. Actors: Micheline Presle, Alfred Adam, Jean Brochard, Pierre Palau, Berthe Bovy, Denis d'Inès, Louis Salou, Sinoël, Suzet Maïs, Roger Karl, Jim Gérald, Gabrielle Fontan.

2. Christian-Jaque, the most prolific French director, was born in 1904 in Paris. Between 1932 and 1939 he directed a great many films, including: *L'Hôtel du Libre Echange, Monsieur Personne, La Maison d'en Face, Un de la Légion, François Premier, Ernest le Rebelle, Les Perles de la Couronne* (in collaboration with Sacha Guitry), *Les Pirates du Rail, Les Disparus de Saint-Agil, Raphaël le Tatoué, Le Grand Elan, L'Enfer des Anges.* During the war he made *L'Assassinat du Père Noël,*

Premier Bal, La Symphonie Fantastique, Carmen, Voyage sans Espoir, and *Sortilèges.*

3. A little later, André Bazin was to discover to his amusement and surprise that the analogy he had spotted between *Boule de Suif* and *Stagecoach* worked in both directions. Indeed, in 1946 it was learned that the Ernest Haycox story "Stage to Lordsburg," which was adapted by Dudley Nichols to become *Stagecoach,* had been directly inspired by Guy de Maupassant's story "Boule de Suif"! (F.T.)

René Chanas' Le Jugement Dernier

Decidedly, the Resistance is not lending itself to treatment by the cinema. René Chanas' *Le Jugement Dernier* [1] is another proof of this.

One of its principal faults is certainly due to the much too facile uprooting that consisted in transposing the action to a "country in Central Europe." The use of actors as popular as Brochard, Vitold, or Bussières makes this transposition pointless, if not irritating. As for the scenario, it contained at least one interesting character—that of the traitor who later tries to die with his comrades and ends by returning to surrender to them and committing suicide before their very eyes. But the idea is treated with an excessive eloquence, and complicated by a Corneillian love story involving the son of the informer and the daughter of his victim.

Nevertheless, this is not a work without interest; in it can be recognized, in what is both good and bad, the character of those films in which the director is his own scenarist: a personal tone and a less anonymous technique than is usual, worthwhile achievements alongside obvious faults of taste. Jeanson's [2] dialogue is not among his best, but it was difficult to do the dialogue for so unequal a scenario without skirting the ridiculous. The actors perform their roles very honestly, especially that of the traitor, but Brochard is miscast as the character he plays.

(*Le Parisien Libéré*—January 1, 1946)

Notes

1. *Le Jugement Dernier.* Direction and scenario: René Chanas. Dialogue: Henri Jeanson. Actors: Michèle Martin, Jean Davy, Raymond Bussières, Louis Seigner, Michel Vitold, Jean Brochard, Jean Desailly.

2. At the end of 1943, Henri Jeanson, twice arrested and then freed by the Gestapo, was prohibited from writing for the cinema. It was therefore under the mocking pseudonym of M. Privey [a pun on the word "privé"—"deprived"] that he wrote his 1944 works, for example, *Farandole,* directed by one of Jean Renoir's former assistants, André Zwoboda. None of this prevented Henri Jeanson from being harassed by the Comité d'Epuration du Cinéma after the Liberation, or from later spreading political calumnies about Jean Renoir, Georges Sadoul, or others! (F.T.)

A tale of the Resistance, *Le Jugement Dernier* (1946) focused on a traitor who tries to atone by surrendering to his comrades. "Decidedly the Resistance is not lending itself to treatment by the cinema," Bazin concluded. (French Cultural Services)

René Clément's La Bataille du Rail

It cannot be said that up to now the Resistance has been a very happy inspiration for French cinema. From *Boule de Suif* to *Le Jugement Dernier,* nothing that has come out of our studios has been more than respectable nor able to approach either the Russian films or the admirable *La Dernière Chance,* which recently came out of Switzerland. It is only fair to note, however, that in relation to these countries France is suffering from a significant production lag. It has been scarcely more than a year since the first scenarios dealing with the Resistance went before the cameras in France. There is no reason not to hope for better films. Finally, however, thanks to René Clément, we are now able to offer the world a film worthy of its subject: *La Bataille du Rail.*[1]

Originally conceived as a documentary, *La Bataille du Rail,* even in its expanded form, claims only to reconstitute the psychological and material conditions of the job of sabotage carried out in the rear areas of the Normandy front by railway workers after the Allied landings. Trains have to be kept from moving, or at the very least have to be delayed. Any means will do: deliberate switching errors, current cuts along the power lines, sabotage of equipment, derailments, coordination with the action of the maquis. But the Germans laboriously repair the spiderweb thread by thread, and it is constantly all to be done over again.

Bested by this intangible enemy that divines his thoughts and undoes his plans, the German is out of his depth and turns nasty. He constantly threatens to shoot people. Sometimes this is actually done to hostages chosen at random. In vain. What can be done in the face of the heroism of an engineer who knowingly derails his train? Nothing can prevent this insectlike gnawing away at each thread of the net-

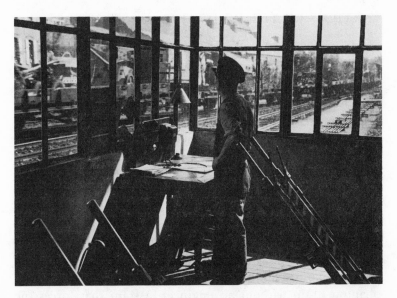

A more successful treatment of the Resistance was *La Bataille du Rail,* which dealt in a semidocumentary fashion with sabotage by French railway workers. Most of the actors were nonprofessionals. (French Cultural Services)

work. A little sawing on the link of a chain, a loosened bolt —and hours and hours are lost, hundreds of tons of supplies fail to reach the front in time.

René Clément and his cameraman, Alekan, were dealing with particularly cinematic material. From *L'Entrée du Train en Gare de La Ciotat* to Renoir's *La Béte Humaine,* by way of *The Great Train Robbery* (1903) and Abel Gance's *La Roue,* the locomotive and the rail have been privileged themes of cinema.

This is no doubt because they unite the rhythmic poetry of the machine, which perhaps only the camera has expressed, with the fundamental movement in filming: the dolly shot. René Clément, whose career has just begun, actually has a rail documentary to his credit. He knows how to make use of the dizzying flight of a roadbed or the rhythm of a connecting rod. This time the French National Railway System made a supplementary and sensational contribution: the actual derailment of a train loaded with tanks. Simultaneously filmed by fourteen cameras shooting from different distances and angles, the shots of the accident could be carefully chosen from 2,500 meters of film that correspond to the few dozen seconds of the event itself. Needless to say, such filmmaking is unique in the annals of cinema.

But the filmmakers have drawn more than a formal and mechanical advantage from their subject. The image constantly engages our interest by relating to the Resistance itself, to the anxious psychology of the saboteur, to the detailed and almost detective story-like development of the plot. That image has also been able to attain to a poetry that is sometimes cruel, and sometimes of a gentleness or humor as absurd and familiar as death. I am thinking of that phantom train without an engineer, a train that forces the switch at the point it should have jumped the tracks and wanders about the countryside on an abandoned stretch of track much to the terror of both men and beasts; or perhaps of that execution of six hostages as the lacerating whistles toll; or of many other happy effects worthy of the greatest Russian films.

It is not without some hesitation that I would nevertheless like to point out several faults to which I attach importance only because of the exceptional qualities of this work. These faults represent the slim margin by which the film fails to achieve the unity of style of a masterpiece.

Originally conceived as a partially narrated documentary, it seems that the film has suffered from having been stretched out. In most cases, a 2,400-meter film cannot do without a story. Here the plot is both insufficient in its dramatic construction and somewhat confused in its development. The film no longer has the nakedness of the documentary but is nevertheless unable to decide to interest us primarily in the characters and their story. No doubt Clément wanted to retain for the actors the egalitarian anonymity of the original action.

Perhaps what was needed was to have the dramatic tension which could not come from a simple plot centered on two or three characters, replaced by a spiritual unity that would have given each image in the film its deep and in some way metaphysical meaning. I will add that cameraman Alekan's tendency toward velvety, almost sensuous, photography also somewhat detracts from the film's unity. Photography that is gray, uniform, and harsh, closer to actuality, like the work of cameraman Page in André Malraux's film *L'Espoir,* would have suited the subject better.

But I repeat that these reservations bear only on the narrow margin that separates *La Bataille du Rail* from perfection. In closing I should like to point out that this film possesses to a rare degree a quality against which nothing prevails: artistic honesty. René Clément [2] has treated a great subject with an intellectual modesty, a tact, and a simplicity that command esteem and straightaway provoke warm support. It is not only a film that one admires, it is a film that one loves and that makes us feel we know and love the auteur like a friend. (*Gavroche*—January 31, 1946)

Notes

1. Producer: Coopérative Générale du Film Français with the collaboration of the "Résistance-Fer" group and the Commission Militaire Nationale. Filmed with the help of the French National Railway System. Direction: René Clément. Scenario: René Clément. Dialogue: Colette Audry. Cameraman: Henri Alekan. Music: Yves Baudrier. Railway Technical Advisor: André Delage. Actors: Antoine Laurent (Camargue), Desagneau (operations chief), Leroy (station master), Redon (engineer), Pauléon (captive railwayman), Rauzena (shunter), Mme Salina, Lozach, Jean Clarieux, Woll, Jean Daurand (other railway workers). Length: 1 hour 20 minutes. Grand Prix du Cinéma Français (1946). Grand Prix du Festival de Cannes (1946).

2. René Clément, born in 1913 in Bordeaux began as a cameraman on short subjects before doing a documentary: *L'Arabie Interdite* (1937). Other short subjects followed: *La Grande Chartreuse, Soigne Ton Gauche* (with Jacques Tati), *La Bièvre, Le Triage* (1938–39), *Ceux du Rail, La Grande Pastorale, Chefs de Demain* (1940–43). *La Bataille du Rail* is his first feature-length film.

Henri Calef's Jéricho

The underground war is already too distant from us for a film to benefit from that passion which would have blinded us to its weaknesses, but the scars that it left in our memories are still so painful that they cannot tolerate being touched uselessly or indecisively. A film about the Resistance must henceforth be perfect. The honesty and talent that might be saluted elsewhere are insufficient qualities for the treatment of such a subject. Until now, only *La Bataille du Rail,* despite its late release, was able to unite sufficient humility and grandeur to justify its undertaking.

It was hoped that even if *Jéricho* ¹ was not quite as successful, it would at least be of a somewhat comparable stature. As it turns out, we are offered a good job that would undoubtedly be fine with any other dramatic scenario but that can now only strike us as irritating and superfluous.

The adaptation of the scenario is based on a true event: the bombing of the Amiens prison by RAF Mosquitos in order to help political prisoners escape. I don't know if the relation between this aerial attack and the imminent execution of 50 hostages is exact, but if it isn't, it would have had to be invented to give the incident a dramatic timespan. Be that as it may, this element of the action is in itself purely external. Consequently, the scenarist only introduced it in the last part of the film, and he tried to fill it out with a psychological action: the last night of the hostages. The moral and physical reactions of men awaiting their death are combined by "parallel editing" with the preparations, the takeoff, and the arrival of the English squadron.

Unlike *La Bataille du Rail,* which deliberately chose to be not only a human document but also a technical one, *Jéricho* aims to capture the psychological and social aspect of the Resistance. The basis of the film is in the life together of men of different origins and temperaments who are united in the same cell by the chance factor of German repression. How will this doctor, this civil servant, this beggar, this land-owner, this blackmarketeer, react to the solidarity of danger and humiliation, to the fraternity of death?

Whereas René Clément used almost nothing but the cam-era to relate facts and give them their meaning, Henri Calef must on the contrary grant great importance to words. The responsibility for the film therefore lies especially with Charles Spaak.

Unfortunately, his dialogue is neither simple enough nor brilliant enough. It remains terribly conventional, despite its falsely authentic air. Charles Spaak is too intelligent a man not to have seen which stereotypes to avoid and what tone not to take; he therefore remains within a secondary convention that avoids vulgarity but gives the entire film an irredeemably false tone. Like a watermark, the intentions of the dialogue seem always visible, and the heavy-handed skill with which the dialogue avoids the shoals merely calls at-tention to it.

Ordinarily, Charles Spaak is one of our best dialoguists, but I don't believe that he is the kind to predominate in a film, as Prévert does. Not the least of Clément's merits is that he knew how to take refuge in silence when words could only be indecent. One has only to compare the sober and silent execution of the hostages in *La Bataille du Rail* with the interminable chattering in *Jéricho*.

The direction of Henri Calef, whose debut [2] I believe this to be, is not lacking in vigor and intelligence. The con-tinuity is perhaps sometimes a little too emphatic. Its quali-ties would be better appreciated if they did not in spite of everything remain inadequate to the subject. Everything re-lating to the sabotaging of the gasoline train parked in the station is very good (actually, the dialogue and scenario are much better here).[3]

It is difficult to think well of actors when one feels that the sentiments they are made to express do not achieve the right tone. Pierre Brasseur, in his role as the cowardly, small-time blackmarket cheat, manages to be bad.

(*Gavroche*—March 21, 1946)

Notes

1. *Jéricho* (1946). Direction: Henri Calef. Scenario: Claude Heymann. Dialogue: Charles Spaak. Photography: Claude Renoir. Producer: Sacha Gordine. Actors: Pierre Brasseur, Pierre Larquey, Jean Brochard, René Génin, Yves Deniaud, Louis Seigner, Line Noro, Raymond Pellegrin, Jean d'Yd, Roland Armontel, Pierre Palau, Henri Nassiet.

2. Henri Calef, born in Bulgaria in 1910, had been an assistant to Berthomieu and Pierre Cheval before making his first film in 1944, *L'Extravagante Mission,* which was followed by *Jéricho.*

3. Thanks to circumstances, Charles Spaak had an insider's view of the prisoners' dialogue. Arrested by the Gestapo in 1943, he wrote the adaptation of *Les Caves du Majestic,* directed by Richard Pottier, while in a prison cell at Fresnes; it was the last French production of the German firm Continentale! (F.T.)

Yves Allégret's Les Démons de l'Aube

Thirty men in a commando unit are assigned to mount stealthy and bloody raids [1] on the North African coast and then in the south of France. In the past, because of a woman, the lieutenant in charge had been guilty of serious negligence during the Resistance. The man who was almost the victim of it has not forgiven him, and by chance the two men find themselves in the same unit. Heroism and danger bring them together, and they die reconciled in mutual esteem.

Such a subject is enough to make us fear the worst (indeed the advertising posters invite these fears by their bad taste), and director Yves Allégret, who began with Viviane Romance's *La Boîte aux Rêves*,[2] doesn't seem to have been of sufficient stature to save this scenario from the reefs that lie in wait for films about the war and the Resistance. Evidently Yves Allégret has not yet had the opportunities he merits.

Director Yves Allégret was unable to steer *Les Démons de l'Aube* away from the reefs that threaten Resistance films. As an officer in a North African commando unit, Georges Marchal gave a superior performance. (French Cultural Services)

Les Démons de l'Aube is a very sympathetic film and in spots even remarkable—badly told, no doubt, and ambiguous in the details; but this very fault, habitual in Allégret, is here a plus for the film, which draws from it a sort of allusive and suggestive style.

Georges Marchal completely rescues his role as the lieutenant from stereotype, and often manages to give him an unhoped-for solidity. The rest of the cast, little-known young actors, is from all points of view worthy of praise.

(*Le Parisien Libéré*—May 12, 1946)

Notes

1. *Les Démons de l'Aube* (1946). Direction: Yves Allégret. Scenario, adaptation, dialogue: Maurice Aubergé and Jean Ferry. Sets: Georges Wakhévitch. Music: Arthur Honegger. Actors: Georges Marchal, Simone Signoret, André Valmy, Dominique Nohain, Marcel Lupovici.

2. Viviane Romance, who had conceived the original idea for *La Boîte aux Rêves*, had initially recruited director Jean Choux (*Jean de la Lune*) before firing him, and then called in Yves Allégret (the younger brother of Marc), whose second directorial assignment (1943) this was; the first, *Tobie Est un Ange* (1941), was never released, the negative of the film having burned in a laboratory. (F.T.)

Louis Daquin's Patrie

It was a praiseworthy idea, treating the Resistance from the perspective of the sixteenth century. The attraction of this interpretation is easy to understand: to strip the subject of what is too accidental in its modern expression and, at the same time, to ground its meaning on the authority of history. Unless I am mistaken, the traditional reticence of French classical art and our taste for moralizing are undoubtedly the reason why France is the only country to have made Resistance films under the cover of an historic alibi: *Boule de Suif* and, now, *Patrie*.[1]

But why have Louis Daquin and his dialoguist Charles Spaak ostensibly attempted to re-create a meticulous present precisely when their scenario permitted them to rise above it? I don't believe that the film has profited from the systematic deliberateness of the allusions to events of the French Resistance. It was not indispensable to have the Prince of Orange, come to deliver the city from the occupation by the troops of the Duke of Alba, make comments that might well have come from General de Gaulle a year ago. A year ago, I say, because it is through this that the immanent justice of the muse of history punishes filmmakers. Because it wanted to be contemporary, the film is now six months too old. Louis Daquin cannot gainsay this.

The Pierre Bost adaptation of Victorien Sardou's Corneillian melodrama—the conflict between duty and love, or rather between public duty and private life—the character of that woman who exists only for her happiness and who sells out her country to save her lover in spite of himself, and the austere fraternity of the clandestine struggle honestly and skillfully avoid the stereotypes that might have been feared.

Louis Daquin's direction doesn't manage to lend an always unquestionable life to this schematicized work through which the didactic intention too often shows. However, the last scenes of the film—the ones in which the insurgents are executed—are not lacking in a nobility of tone, a poetry, and an authentically epic grandeur.

Pierre Blanchar plays his role exactly as the tone of the film demands. He wasn't the man to have attenuated its faults. Jean Desailly is, alas, very bad in an obviously difficult role. Maria Mauban honorably takes on her unpleasant part.

(*Le Parisien Libéré*—October 25, 1946)

Notes

1. *Patrie* (1946) from a play by Victorien Sardou. Direction: Louis Daquin. Adaptation: Pierre Bost. Dialogue: Charles Spaak. Photography: André Bac, Nicolas Hayer. Sets: René Moulaert. Music: Jean Wiener. Actors: Pierre Blanchar, Lucien Nat, Pierre Dux, Jean Desailly, Maria Mauban, Julien Bertheau, Louis Seigner, Pierre Asso, Marcel Lupovici.

5 : THE FIRST CANNES FESTIVAL

The Cannes Festival of 1946

Those who might have believed that the Cannes International Film Festival would be a parade of masterpieces would have been greatly mistaken. As it turned out, those privileged to attend the Festival have seen fewer good films than an alert weekly filmgoer can find in six months on the Champs-Elysées alone. From July to September the first-run houses have shown: *Citizen Kane, The Little Foxes,*[1] *The Westerner,*[2] *How Green Was My Valley,*[3] *Double Indemnity,*[4] *The Woman in the Window*[5]; with the exception of Billy Wilder's *The Lost Weekend,* the screen of the Casino de Cannes was far from being graced with American works of that same quality. From among the rest of world film production there stand out five or six films the making of which fills a definite need: *La Bataille du Rail,*[6] *Open City,*[7] *La Dernière Chance,*[8] *Brief Encounter,*[9] *La Symphonie Pastorale,*[10] *Maria Candelaria,*[11] and perhaps also *The Earth Will Be Red, Tournant Décisif, The Captive Heart.* Add two or three other honest films like *Le Père Tranquille,* or interesting ones like *Croc Blanc,* and you more or less have the balance sheet of what one "had to" and what one "could" see of 1945–46 world film production (and even then, several of these go back to before 1945). Since most of the films I've mentioned, will be commercially released, if we consider only the intrinsic value of the works shown at the Festival, those film lovers who were unable to go to Cannes and be regularly admitted to the Casino can easily console themselves.

It is doubtful that the best films made in the world were presented at Cannes. This becomes quite clear if we merely note that France preferred to offer *Le Revenant*[12] rather than *Farrebique.*[13] But it is even doubtful that the best of the rejected world film production would have basically changed the physiognomy of the Festival. A barren year? No doubt. Neither Wyler, nor Capra, nor John Ford, nor Preston Sturges, nor Carné, nor Renoir, nor Eisenstein. But let's not have any illusions. The first lesson to be drawn from the Cannes Festival is this: out of two or three thousand full-length films produced in the world every year, there are perhaps only about fifteen whose titles are worth remembering, a half dozen that are worthy of mention in the future histories of cinema.

If the Cannes Festival had been nothing more than a parade of more or less interesting films, its success would have been slight. But the intrinisic value of the films is not the only thing of importance here. The interest of such an event—and that interest is undeniable—seems to me to reside principally in the opportunity it provides to establish comparisons. An international if not a universal art thanks to its very technique, cinema is paradoxically the most national art when it comes to its commercial exploitation. The economic or political causes of this are so obvious that they need not be insisted on here.

In short, while a well-stocked book store has on its shelves enough foreign translations and recent magazines to make it possible to follow contemporary international literature, only congresses like that in Cannes make it possible to form an idea about world film production. From this point of view the geological cross-section made in cinema by the Festival was fascinating to those interested in knowing where cinematic art and industry are heading. The vantage points from which it is possible to make a comparative analysis of various national productions are too numerous for us to be restricted to the arbitrary choice of four or five of them. Let us talk first of the subjects.

One of these is common to all the European countries that experienced occupation by the Germans: the Resistance. No less than three of the six films presented by France were on this theme: *La Bataille du Rail, Le Père Tranquille,* and *Patrie.* Italy showed *Open City;* Czechoslovakia, *Men Without Wings;* Denmark, *The Earth Will Be Red;* and Russia, *Zoïa.* Not all these films are masterpieces, but none is unimportant. Europe during the Occupation unquestionably lived through a European experience that every man in every country immediately understands. The hatred of the oppressor, the dangers of underground activity, the techniques of sabotage or of torture, are an international dialect that needs no subtitles or dubbing. The Resistance constitutes a common mythology, the national variants of which do not significantly modify the archtype.

The French films do not come off too badly in this confrontation but it is interesting to note some of their individual features. First the variety of tone. *Patrie* is an historical film with elaborate sets and costumes; *Le Père Tranquille* is a long and charming cabaret sketch; *La Bataille du Rail* is a realistic documentary.

The foreign films, at least those shown in Cannes, are all dramas, practically documentaries. They are all marked by violence and atrocity. But if the variety of tone and genre of the French films is greater, the foreign works have gone further than ours when it comes to a human realism. No French director has dared show what was nevertheless the dominant fact about underground activity: torture. In France this seems to be a secret and sacred theme that art can at most evoke through allusion, ellipsis, and indirection. And no doubt we were right for us, but the others could risk it and have succeeded. The torture scene of *Open City* is a seamless and natural extension of the sober and vigorous realism of the action. In *The Earth Will Be Red,* the smashed hands of the hero make us momentarily turn our eyes away, but we do not question the necessity of the shot in the development of the film. The rotting corpses piled up in Buchenwald were like that. It is doubtful if such descriptions would have been possible in literature without falling into turgidity or sadism. And yet how much stronger the cinematic image is. But cinema is the art of reality.

The war and the Resistance confer on European cinema a climate that profoundly distinguishes it from American productions. A phenomenology of death in contemporary cinema will have to be established.

There is a great deal of dying on the world's screens in 1946. But it isn't so much of the quantity that I am thinking —Hollywood screen characters are also dying—as of the significance of the death. In Europe the deaths on the screen concern the spectator. In American they are imaginary. They are "movie" deaths. There exists between European films and the European public a common affective denominator that seems more and more absent from American films.

Think, for example, of a film like Fritz Lang's *The Woman in the Window,* which might have been a horrifying crime tragedy if in the end it hadn't been carefully evaporated in a dream. In not one of the American films presented at Cannes can the spectator feel himself in the least "concerned," involved by the subject and by the characters (except, perhaps, in *The Lost Weekend*). It would be wrong to believe that it is the scenario that distinguishes escapist cinema from realist cinema. There are war documentaries and newsreels that are more "escapist" than fantasy films, and vice-versa. The American films, with only a few exceptions and regardless of their scenario, seem suspended in a stratosphere in which problems of individual or collective life, of morality, or of politics are invoked only in the imagination, like death in a detective novel. The world in which the characters struggle is separated from us by a glass that their blood does not penetrate.

The causes of this "irrealism" of American cinema seem various. Perhaps not the least of them is the disastrous influence of the Hays-Johnson office, which exercises a censorship that is above all moral and prevents a subject from ever being treated in depth and in all its consequences. But it is to be feared that responsibility must also be borne by an automatic noninstitutional censorship, a sociological censorship aimed at seeing to it that the public is never really upset.

What I dislike about most of the American scenarios is equaled only by my enthusiasm for their mise-en-scène. We've come to the end of the myth of a standardized Hollywood in which anonymous technical crews pre-masticate the director's work so that he is unable to express himself in his own style. The formidable Hollywood machinery seems to have finally achieved that degree of perfection which frees the artist from technical concerns. A director now thinks in cinema with a variety and precision of syntax and vocabulary that are equal to that of writing. As a result we see a multiplication of the names of directors whose presence in the credits signifies something.

I am speaking not only of an Orson Welles or a Preston Sturges—who because they are able to be their own scenarists even escape our general charges against American scenarios—but of a Billy Wilder, an Alfred Hitchcock, an Otto Preminger, a Clifford Odets, or even a Robert Siodmak or a George Stevens, who seemed to be devoted to mass production. Along with the five or six great veterans (Ford, Capra, Wyler, etc.), there are now some fifteen names that one must know to orient oneself in Hollywood production. The films shown at Cannes were, as to their subjects, rather uniformly disappointing (except for *The Lost Weekend* and *Wonder Man*), but they could not be accused of monotony of form. Their styles were certainly as different as those of a half dozen novels by strong personalities.

If in addition we consider the increasing influence of books on American production, the multiplication of adaptations of novels and the almost complete disappearance of original scenarios, we are forced to the conclusion that cinema is in the sociological and esthetic situation of producing for the screen the equivalent of books.

Not that books are disappearing—on the contrary—but a work of fiction simply tends to inevitably reproduce itself in the cinema (to some extent in the theater as well). Take, for example, *Of Mice and Men;* supposing that the film is as good as the novel, are we dealing with a play, a book, or a film? I see in it an esthetic trinity, a single work in three arts. When the cinematic culture of writers is more widespread, theoretically there will be nothing to prevent the novelist of the future from writing his work simultaneously in cinema and in literature, just as Malraux did with *L'Espoir*. But *L'Espoir*-film still has the awkwardness of the amateur (of genius). Hollywood, on the contrary, is able to furnish the exact cinematic equivalent of a paragraph by Faulkner, by Hemingway, or by Caldwell. For several years now we have been watching the puberty of the American cinematic imprint.

Unfortunately, a vigilant censorship still protects this adolescent art against forming the dangerous companionships risked by the other muses. If it is allowed to read the same stories, it is only after the text has been expurgated and love replaced by dove, *ad usum Delphini*. As a result, we still see this grown-up and perfectly constituted art dulling its mind on scenarios which it has outgrown.

Fortunately, from time to time it happens that Orson Welles, William Wyler, Preston Sturges, and recently Clifford Odets provide the cinema with material worthy of it, that a scenario seeks out and finds its form instead of having a uselessly original form search for the scenario for which it was made (as, for example, in most of Hitchcock's films). Can we look forward to the day when the moral and economic guardians, which are all that keeps American cinema in an artificial infantilism, will sufficiently relax their controls? We

would then, perhaps, see the birth of a cinematic production in every way worthy of American literary production.
(*Le Courrier de l'Etudiant*—October 30–November 13, 1946)

Notes

1. Directed by William Wyler.
2. Directed by William Wyler.
3. Directed by John Ford.
4. Directed by Billy Wilder.
5. Directed by Fritz Lang.
6. Directed by René Clément.
7. Directed by Roberto Rossellini.
8. Directed by Léopold Lindberg.
9. Directed by David Lean.
10. Directed by Jean Delannoy.
11. Directed by Emilio Fernandez.
12. Directed by Christian-Jaque, scenario and dialogue by Henri Jeanson.
13. Directed by Georges Rouquier; the roles were performed by actual farmers.

6 : MALRAUX'S *L'ESPOIR*

On L'Espoir, *or Style in the Cinema*

There have already been many critical articles justly emphasizing the relationship between the book and the film, focusing on the very substance of the work, its intrinsic value, and its reactivation due to contemporary events; coming somewhat late on the scene, I can only repeat these judgments. But *L'Espoir* [1] is a work of sufficient stature to support the examination of details. I will therefore consider as established the almost unanimous reviews that followed the film's release at the Max-Linder theater and will restrict myself to some comments on style which I feel should be pursued in depth.

It is no accident that Malraux is the contemporary writer who has spoken best about the cinema. The fact is that there are basic affinities between his style and the language of the screen. I think that he is the first to have pointed out the role of ellipsis in the cinema and the growing place of this figure of rhetoric in the contemporary novel (and especially in his own). In practice, however, this affinity reveals a confusion that one would not have suspected *a priori*.

Ellipsis in Malraux's film may perhaps be no less effective and esthetically significant than in the book, but it does not penetrate the image without doing it violence. I believe that this unexpected resistance of cinematic expression to the transcription of an elliptical art can throw light on an important point about literary and cinematic stylistics.

In this very publication Claude-Edmonde Magny * has analyzed in depth the significance of the ellipsis in contemporary literature: to destroy the possibility of connection, to introduce nothingness between the objects and the instants. No

---

* These views appear in *The Age of the American Novel: The Film Aesthetic of Fiction between the Wars* (New York, 1972). —Trans.

doubt the metaphysic of the ellipsis is not the same in Malraux, Camus, or Faulkner, for example. All contemporary novelists, however, share a desire to introduce into the story by means of ellipsis a discontinuity that is simultaneously temporal and spatial, capable of preventing our minds from automatically organizing reality according to a certain logic of appearances, of giving it a meaning. More than any other, Malraux's esthetic proceeds by a discontinuous choice of instants. The thread of the story is deliberately broken. Only a few shattered links mark the passage of an action that even the attentive reader is not always able to reconstruct perfectly.

Now it seems that cinema does not tolerate discontinuity. In spite of a structure broken into "shots," the cinematic story more and more tends to spare us ruptures. The term *découpage,* used in the professional jargon to indicate the succession of shots planned before the making of the film, is a misconstruction. Americans more rightly say "continuity." The need for a smooth and unfragmented linkage of one shot to another can indeed be found in the term *raccord* [continuity shot]. Literary ellipsis introduces a gap into reality, a gap which the reader can bridge intellectually but which is painful to the mind of the film spectator.

I see at least two obvious reasons for this: our state of passivity in relation to the image—that is, our natural reluctance when confronted by the screen to make an intellectual effort—and the uniform unreeling of the images. It is the image and not the intermediate relay of the intelligence that must directly set our imagination going. Despite the spectator's good will and courage, the intelligence is actually hindered by the irreversibility of the spectacle. An obscure sentence is reread; an over-elliptical film sequence is lost definitively. It appears that the cinematic ellipsis, in order to appeal only to our imagination, must remain plastic, more spatial than temporal. A murder may be represented in the cinema by a hand loosening its hold on a telephone receiver. This gesture-sign remains in direct and contemporaneous relation with the action it suggests; it does not break the continuity. The real gaps of the cinematic tale are rarely felt as ellipses.

A man gets out of a car and enters his house. The following shot shows him going into his room. The ascent of the stairs, the walk down the hallway, etc., would in reality have been an unnecessary overtaxing of the modern spectator. If the logic of the drama demands it, however, the director can intentionally use this objective description as a pathetic pleonasm (when, for example, we know that the man is going to find his wife murdered). In *L'Espoir*-film, when the disfigured pilot asks Magnin if he has a mirror, we see the captain open his wallet as though to look, begin to draw from it a little round mirror, replace it, and reply: No.

We can see from this example the necessary work of intelligence that must reconstruct the moral motives, which are not expressed plastically. Of course, here the ellipsis, intellectual though it may be, is still easily comprehensible; but in other cases the limit of attention is crossed.

The critics and even the makers of the film attribute its obscurity to external circumstances: the many shots that could not be filmed. Obviously, it cannot be said that the film wouldn't have been clearer if it had been possible to follow the scenario exactly. However, I nevertheless believe that in the final analysis even the accidental gaps play exactly the same role as the deliberate ellipses. Any other film would have been ruined under these conditions. Here, on the contrary, the gaps contribute to the unity of style and bring the film closer to the book, which in reality is no less obscure. Because Malraux's ellipses appeal to the intelligence more than to the imagination, they are very unequally understood. I have several times been present when the film was shown to a relatively intellectual audience, and I have always been struck by the fact that certain scenes seem either clear or obscure without any apparent reason.

The murder of the fascist innkeeper by the peasant, for example, was understood by some and remained mysterious to others. It was not that those who failed to understand were more stupid than the others but that the speed of their attention, the particular psychology of their perception, did not allow for a sufficiently rapid intervention of their intelligence. There has been much criticism of the "explanatory" intertitles that now accompany the film, and it has been said that they uselessly paraphrase the action without clarifying anything. Now, this text was worked out by Denis Marion after his investigations following several showings of the film to so-called "cultivated" spectators. It was inevitable that these explanations would satisfy no one, since under these conditions the "obscurity" of the shots is eminently subjective and linked to individual psychology. No referendum could resolve the problem.

This is why Malraux's film remains very literary—not because of the abundance or the tone of the dialogue, not even because of the scenario or the psychology of the characters, but paradoxically because of what should have been most cinematic: the use of a visual ellipsis in which the film in reality retains the intellectual structure of a literary ellipsis.

This observation is, however, not necessarily a regret. There is no denying that this violence to the laws of cinema has a positive side to it. The tension imposed on our minds, the kind of esthetic sadism or cruelty involved in this struggle with the imagination, the very obscurity of many passages, confer a sometimes dazzling aura on the film. But these are perhaps over-intellectual pleasures, valuable no doubt, but not in the warp of cinematic art conceived of as "necessarily" popular. The merchants who refused the film might have been excused if they had not also been unaware of the element of achievement about it, an achievement to which they are so little accustomed that they no longer even recognize it: grandeur and authenticity. But I have promised to speak only of the style!

By itself, of course, ellipsis does not define Malraux and his style. To it must at least be added comparison. A rapid statistical study of his syntactic vocabulary would bring out the frequent use of the conjunction "like" or the pure and simple opposition which is only the ellipsis of this conjunction. Malraux's language is highly imaged. His descriptions are almost permanent comparisons. What follows are two quotes from a short paragraph taken from the episode of the attack on the big gun by Puig's car. "Behind him in a gasping howl of horns and claxons two Cadillacs were coming up with the sweeping zigzag of gangster films. . . . Black debris in the midst of bloodstains, a fly squashed on a wall." "The sweating militiamen fired away in a furnace-room atmosphere, their naked torsos ocellated with spots of light like panthers with black spots."

An analysis of the meaning of comparisons in Malraux would lead us to a simultaneous study of what might rather vaguely be labeled "rapprochement." The comparison is itself basically only a rapprochement of the concrete and the imaginary on the basis of a resemblance. But doesn't the antithesis itself contain a subjective resemblance for the mind? Malraux uses images—real or imaginary—as a decor designed to give the action or the object described its esthetic or metaphysical illumination. Whether he tells us that the attacking militiamen swarming into the square fell "like" game, or whether he shows these militiamen . . . making rise before them a flight of pigeons, men and birds strewing the ground, hit by the same machinegun bullets, the rapprochement, by imaginary resemblance or inscribed in reality, has the same basic significance for the writer.

"One can analyze," writes Malraux in *Psychologie du Cinéma,* "the mise-en-scène of a great novelist, whether his object be the narration of facts, the portrayal or the analysis of character, or even an interrogation on the meaning of life, whether his talent tends to a proliferation, like that of Proust, or a crystalization, like that of Hemingway, he is led to relate—in other words to summarize and put on stage— in other words to make present. I call the mise-en-scène of a novelist the instinctive or premeditated choice of instants to which he is drawn and the means he uses to give them a particular importance."

To make present and give a meaning to, can only be, in an artist, one and the same action, since the presence is only justified in terms of the meaning he gives it. Now, in Malraux the writer, this meaning is illuminated in two principal ways: the first logical—discourse and dialogues, often very intellectual, in which the characters participate; the other, which I will call esthetic—the meaning that derives implicitly from the comparisons or the rapprochements. Whether these be imaginary or concrete, their value is exactly the same. He will write, for example: "Behind Garcia, on the outstretched arm of an apostle, machinegun bands dried like laundry. He hung his leather jacket on the extended index finger." The imaginary and antithetical comparison of the first sentence plays exactly the same role in the "mise-en-scène" as the equally antithetical but concrete rapprochement of the second sentence.

What can the visual projection on the screen of this literary mise-en-scène be? A necessary first observation: cinema knows only the concrete since its images are objectively real. Its means for indicating the imaginary are extremely limited and of a dubious esthetic value; superimposition, slow motion, negative film, or optical effect being only very rarely acceptable, they cannot be used in a work of this nature. The novel, on the contrary, works only on the imaginary, since real facts or thoughts are transmitted to us by words. It follows that comparison in the formal and classical sense is a specifically literary technique and that the conjunction "like" has no equivalent in cinematic syntax.[2]

An old argument of those contemptuous of cinema claims that it leaves our imagination passive since cinema is obliged to say all. One could find here, if it was still necessary, an additional refutation of their claim. Unable to formulate the image suggested to him by the object he is photographing, the artist is obliged to leave the job of finding that image to the spectator. But what assurance does he have that the spectator will indeed find it or even that it will occur to him to try? Here again the technique and its psychological consequences control the esthetic. The spectator in the movie theater does not have the time to stop and think. The image cannot call on the voluntary intelligence. Its job is only to excite the unstriped muscles of consciousness. The filmmaker has attained his goal when the photographed image spontaneously provokes the desirable associations in us. I say "associations" because in most cases the image is still too involved in reality not to be charged with a certain metaphorical polyvalence. Actually, most often we do not choose from among the possible images—they do not even rise to our consciousness; but their potentiality is obscurely felt and it is this that gives the image its esthetic density. In its narrative aspect cinema is an art of ellipsis, but insofar as plastic reproduction of reality goes, cinema is an art of potential metaphor.

Happily, Malraux has not attempted, as he more or less did when it came to ellipsis, to transcribe the comparison literally; and it can be said that most of his images possess precisely that exciting density which continuously provokes our imagination. No doubt they appeal more to the intelligence than is true in most films, but this appeal is not prohibited so long as the obscure layers of consciousness are also reached. Thus, when the dynamiters leave that grocery or general store, a slight movement of the camera brings to the foreground an enigmatic demijohn into which acid is dripping from a funnel, drop by drop. The intellectual symbolism of this image can lend itself to long commentaries, but the crystalline noise of the drops sounding in the dramatic silence of the room, the waves of their impact on the liquid—the only movement in this immobility deserted by the agitation of men—the very form of the object vaguely evocative of an hourglass, all these details among which the writer would choose and which he would surround by comparisons, are given to us in a raw state charged with meaning by way of the multiple potentials of metaphors. Since we have spontaneously felt these symbols, it matters little that they only crystallize in our minds upon later reflection.

But if literary comparison is forbidden to the screen, the rapprochement of two real facts, drawing a particular importance from their juxtaposition, is on the contrary a privileged technique of cinema. Like the book, the film abounds in these concrete associations: the shot of the faded sunflowers immediately after the murder of the fascist innkeeper; the silence scored by the call of the cicadas following the roar of the plane; the flight of the migratory birds preceding the attack by enemy fighter planes; and above all that unforgettable effect of the ant moving along the machinegun sight.

It can even be said that here cinematic means serve Malraux better than literature does, because of the habitual choice of his rapprochements. In Malraux the reference is generally made from man to nature, to plants, to animals; these references are very often geological or sidereal. The literary evocation thus very certainly lags behind the concrete representation. There are domains in which imagination is almost necessarily inferior to perception (the war documentary gave us abundant proof of that). It is of such things that the inhuman (it might be called cosmic) counterpoint by which Malraux always orchestrates the human action is composed; he has found in the cinema the maximum of expression and of artistic effectiveness.

Nevertheless, there remain here and there implicit comparisons that belong more to literary than to plastic expression. They do not harm the film, and I only mention them as examples in which the ambivalance of Malraux as writer and filmmaker can be caught in action. When one of the machinegunners of the plane is wounded, his comrade shouts to him to make a tourniquet and throws him a first-aid kit: "like a quoit" says the book. Now, in the film, Malraux was clearly obsessed by this comparison. The medical kit is flat, and the actor throws it horizontally. It is impossible for the filmgoer who has reread the book not to think to himself "like a quoit." Another director, who had to make this sequence from the scenario, would probably have retained only its dramatic interest and would not have made an effort to respect an image that could mean nothing to the unalerted spectator. In addition, it can also be seen that sometimes the actors are trying to follow literally the indications in the book, but these intentions are too subtle to be effective on the screen.

It should not be thought, however, that this film incurs the reproach of being "literary" in the usual and generally pejorative sense of the word. The liaison and close parallelism of the two works is most often to the credit of the film. The influence of literature is condemnable in the cinema only when it is at the expense of cinematic expression —for example, when dialogue is substituted for plastic expression or when the director prefers to use words rather than action and the meaningful use of decor and objects to suggest the characters.

Some novelists, to the exact extent that their value is inseparable from language, gain nothing from the cinematic adaptation of their works. The psychology of the characters they create, their drama, the universe in which they live, are determined by the means of analysis offered the artist by literary art. This is evident, for example, in the novel of analysis and introspection in the French tradition.

It is often easy to be mistaken about the cinematic value of such or such a novel: it was only after a half-dozen films that it became obvious that an author like Georges Simenon was not so easy to adapt as had been believed. Certain subjects are in themselves literary, and the films that can be drawn from them will always make us regret the originals. Such is not the case with Malraux's film. Despite a fidelity to the book—a fidelity with which not even the adaptors of Henry Bordeaux's popular novels could be reproached—with some reservations, *L'Espoir* is a film whose originality is as great as that of the book. This is no doubt due to the very art of Malraux, to his writer's mise-en-scène which —except for the long intellectual monologues naturally eliminated on the screen—tends to a passionate observation of men and of things, to a sort of biased and dramatic objectivity that lends itself to visual expression.

However, I would suggest a deeper reason is to be found in the relationship that the artist here maintains with his work. Malraux completely expresses himself in his film and in his book, without any precedence of the one over the other. For him, it is not a question of adaptation but of two creations that absorb him equally. The similitudes that we have emphasized are rather a symmetry in relation to the axis of creation from which Malraux's style branches out equally in two different forms of expression. The experience and temperament of Malraux as writer are undoubtedly at the origin of his characters, which can be challenged from a cinematic point of view; of his ellipses; or of his several symbols; but in its very faults this film gives the impression of a direct creation, as personal as a novel or a painting. We are dealing, in the full sense of the words, with a work and a style.

Style is a quality more rare in the cinema than in the other arts because—since it is the most intimate expression (after handwriting) of the creator's personality—the complexity of techniques and the multiple collaborations thus required, interpose between the director and the work. The never-ending argument about who is the auteur of a film is proof

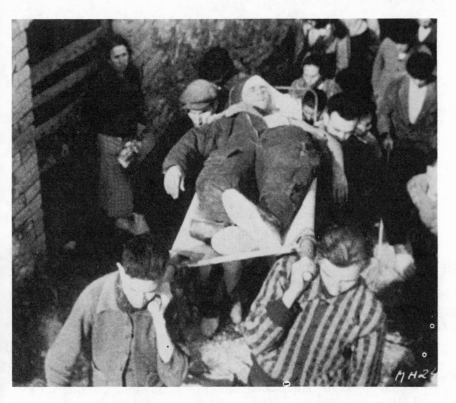

A wounded Loyalist aviator is carried down the mountain in André Malraux's *L'Espoir* (1939), the film version of his novel about the Spanish Civil War. Not seen in France until 1945, it is still under-appreciated. (Museum of Modern Art)

of this. A collective work can have "some" style, but it is almost impossible for the principal maker to impose himself sufficiently on the crew so that the work achieves "a" style as personalized as in the individual arts.

Only the amateur film achieves—paradoxically, thanks to the poverty of its means—a liberty of expression that the heavy machinery of commercial filmmaking does not allow; this was also true of the silent film, which was less dependent on technical factors and in which montage (the absolutely individual moment of creation) played a greater role. Actually, something of amateurism remained in many silent films. We see this clearly in the work of Vigo [3] and it makes us wonder if the decisive crisis of development of the modern director, the one that decides his future health, is not a function of the dissolution of the amateur film into the commercial film.

Grémillon from *Un Tour au Large* to *Remorques;* Carné from *Eldorado du Dimanche* to *Le Jour Se Lève;* René Clair from *Entr'acte* and *La Tour* to *Quatorze Juillet;* Vigo from *A Propos de Nice* to *L'Atalante*. This decisive and often laborious transformation does not come about as chronologically as might be thought; it begins again a little with each film, and a director with several commercial films to his credit will suddenly reveal himself haunted by the amateur work of his youth.

For example, one might wonder if the commercial failure of such excellent films as *Le Crime de Monsieur Lange* or *La Règle du Jeu* couldn't thus be explained. In such cases the amateurism doesn't manifest itself by the poverty of technical aspects or the lack of experience, but in a certain relation of the work to its auteur. Though in commercial filmmaking the director must think only of the public, there is in Renoir's best films a kind of delectation designed for insiders, a complicity of friends who are making a film together for their pleasure. Thus *La Règle du Jeu* has not yet managed to find an audience outside of the ciné clubs, to which it has been confined not only by the censor.

The current evolution of American cinema, which tends to the elimination of individual style and toward more and more anonymous stylistics, is moving in the same direction: the elimination of all traces of amateurism.

The problem where Malraux is concerned is to know to what extent *L'Espoir* remains an inspired amateur film even though it was made in a studio with actors and a professional cameraman. Also, to what extent is the uncertainty of its commercial success linked to this? Will Malraux make other films? What will he accomplish when he has accepted all the exigencies of a cinematic matter that he has until now dominated, forced, with an extraordinary intuition of most of its basic laws? Put another way—what would Malraux accomplish in Hollywood, where Faulkner, Hemingway, and others are already working for the movies? We don't want to see this experiment pushed that far, but we are waiting with an intense curiosity for Malraux to film in Paris—with every available technical resource, without electricity failures and without bombardments—his *La Condition Humaine*.   (*Esprit*—1945)

Notes

1. *L'Espoir* (originally *Sierra de Teruel*). Production: Edouard Corniglion-Molinier. Scenario: André Malraux, assisted by Denis Marion, Spanish translation by Max Aub. Shooting script: Boris Peskine. Direction: André Malraux, assisted by Max Aub and Denis Marion. Photography: Louis Page. Editing: André Malraux, assisted by George Grace. Sets: Vincent Petit. Script Girl: Paule Boutault. Music: Darius Milhaud. Director of Production: Roland Tual. Actors: José Sempere (Commandant Pena), Andres Mejuto (Munoz), Julio Pena (Attignies), Pedro Codina (Schreiner), José Lado (the peasant), Nicolas Rodriguez (Mercery), S. Ferro (Saïdi), Castillo (Gonzalez). Filmed: Barcelona (Montjuich Studio) and exteriors in Catalonia: August 1, 1938–January 1939; Paris (Pathé Studio) and exteriors in France: April 1939. First private showing: July 1939. Public release: Max-Linder Theatre, June 1945. Prix Louis Delluc, December 1945.

2. This affirmation needs to be somewhat qualified. It is not absolutely impossible to translate the comparison to cinema. This technique is abundantly present, for example, in the films of Abel Gance. In *Fury* Fritz Lang follows a shot of chattering gossips with a shot of fowl in a barnyard; the fade that links these two shots is the exact equivalent of the conjunction. However, the real image does not seem to lend itself to this effect. Our minds spontaneously admit the objectivity of the visual image. The transition to the imaginary is thickened, made heavy by the physical presence of the object. The comparison is never without an emphasis, a crude heaviness that most often robs it of all esthetic value. (André Bazin)

3. Banned since 1933, *Zéro de Conduite* was licensed by the censor in 1945 and shown at the Pantheon movie theater with *L'Espoir* in November. It was probably at that time that Bazin discovered the work of Vigo. (F.T.)

Reply by André Malraux to André Bazin

March 8

Monsieur,

I received the study you devoted to my film during a moment of complete chaos. I wanted to reply seriously, not simply to thank you, and the result is that I have not replied at all—until today.

What you have to say about ellipsis is not only subtle but accurate. The uncompleted sequences (half of the film) have nothing to do with this. Except for the large section in the middle (between the dynamiters and the pilots), I have continuously modified the scenario and the dialogue to take into account the approaching catastrophe. Our last scenes were filmed with the guns of FRANCO on the other side of the hills, but they were the last that were absolutely necessary. Sequences are missing; but properly speaking there are no holes in the sequences made. The effect you speak of comes from the style, as you have clearly understood.

As for the reaction of the public (commercially, the film was a semi-failure), it is difficult to nail down, simply because I refused to allow dubbing and a subtitled film only rarely wins a large audience—and when it does it often seems obscure, though spectators faced with the work of a professional, moreover a work obviously completed, are less willing to admit their uneasiness. You speak of a "selected" public; the reaction of the other has been similar.

What you say about my use of the image ("to give the action a metaphysical illumination") also struck me. There is in this domain something between the cinema and the novel: the drama. Shakespeare too annexes the extra-poetic domain (let's call it metaphysical to simplify) by illumination.

You have very clearly seen—and you are the only one, I

believe, at least among the critics—that the suggestive force of the drop of water, after the departure of the dynamitors, comes from the vague identity of form between the demijohn and an hourglass. But remember that poetry too plays on these *données,* and its rapprochements of "irrational" sounds play the same role as the rapprochement of forms does here.

The link (I am following your article) between the comparison in the book and the one in the film ("like a quoit") comes not from the influence of the book but from the obsession, from the force of memory, in both cases. And from a sort of submission to this memory out of a desire to film (and write) *exact* things about war, when they are things that I saw. The war documentary has weakened all that. But remember that this film showed for the first time the interior of a plane, for the first time a multiseat fighter in action.

"The director does not progress in a straight line but in a spiral and returns to the amateur style of his 'youth.' " * Very true, but this is not only true of directors . . .

I will not comment on the essence of your article, which would take us too far and of which we will speak if we one day meet. Please consider this rapid discussion (?), this bit of dialogue, as nothing more than the desire to thank you for the most ingenious and the most attentive study that has been devoted to this film, and accept my warm regards.

André Malraux

I would like, however, to add this—that I am grateful to you for having been the first to point out that what interests me in cinema is the means of linking, artistically, man to the world (as a cosmos) by a means other than language. In the plays of Shakespeare this link is provided by lyricism; in the novel it is provided by the description of an element

* Malraux paraphrases rather than quotes Bazin. —Trans.

external to the character (Tolstoy's images relating to the wounded Prince André after Austerlitz). The camera can always be passed over clouds and the Russians have vulgarized this; but there are sharper and more subtle means. If I were to make another film, its essential images would be of the type of the ant racing over the gonio-sight of the machine-gun—an image you picked up.

Index

Page numbers in italics refer to illustrations.

Never previously collected, these reviews and articles by André Bazin, covering a rich but misunderstood period of French cinema, are doubly important in that they show the critical development of the man who "single-handedly brought the French film back to life" (Pauline Kael).

In an insightful introduction and notes for this newly available material, director François Truffaut provides an overall historical context that incidentally throws an interesting light on aspects of his own triumphant *Le Dernier Métro*, a film set in the German occupation of Paris during World War II.

Despite difficulties caused by material shortages, the flight or imprisonment of major cinema artists, and the harassment of censors, these tragic years demonstrated the vitality of French cinema. They saw the emergence of new talent such as that of Robert Bresson, whose *Les Anges du Péché* Bazin was among the first to hail and the reaffirmation of the cinematic genius of such men as Jean Delannoy and Marcel Carné in works like *L'Eternel Retour* and *Les Visiteurs du Soir*.

But whether he is analyzing a masterpiece or a turkey, Bazin's true topic is cinema itself—its nature, formation, and future. The origins of the *auteur*-based approach to film criticism in Bazin's classic *What Is Cinema?* are clear in such incisive articles as "Let's Rediscover Cinema!," "How Not to See Films," and "Cinema and Popular Art."

The collection also includes a number of surprises, among them André Malraux's detailed commentary on Bazin's analysis of his still underappreciated film adaptation of *L'Espoir,* and